LAYERSOF FLAVORS

RAY OVERTON

Photographs by Jerry Burns

LONGSTREET
Atlanta, Georgia

This book is dedicated to my brother Ricky and my sister Robyn for their simple reassurances, encouragement to follow my dreams and unwavering confidence in my ability to realize those dreams. Thanks guys, I love you!

Published by
LONGSTREET PRESS, INC.
A subsidiary of Cox Newspapers,
A subsidiary of Cox Enterprises, Inc.
2140 Newmarket Parkway
Suite 122
Marietta, GA 30067

Printed in Hong Kong by Paramount Printing
1st printing, 1998
Library of Congress Catalog Card Number: 97-76260
ISBN: 1-56352-464-3

Electronic film prep by Advertising Technologies Incorporated, Atlanta, Georgia

Book and jacket design by Burtch Bennett Hunter

CONTENTS

INTRODUCTION

I have always enjoyed good food—sometimes too much, but then again, who hasn't? Food and its aromas can evoke memories of times past. Every time I smell fresh-perked coffee mingled with the savory aroma of sizzling bacon, my mind escapes to frosty mornings on my Granny Lou's farm in North Carolina, when I used to sit, safe and secure, in the antique rocker by the wood-burning stove. I can remember where I was and at what station in life when I ate my way through such culinary rites of passage as steamed lobster with drawn butter, Beluga caviar, escargot, sushi, sweetbreads, chitterlings, rattlesnake, and alligator. Over the years, this interest in food somehow progressed from an enjoyable hobby to an overwhelming passion. I began to realize that those early years in my grandmother's kitchen had planted the seeds for my career. Eventually, after working as Nathalie Dupree's apprentice and then assistant, I started my own catering company and cooking school. Here, I was able to share what I had learned about food, cooking techniques, and how to make time in the kitchen more than a daily necessity. I had found my calling.

When I was working on my previous cookbook last year, one of the "marketing types" involved in the publication expressed some concern that some of my recipes contained so many ingredients, although she recognized that the recipes themselves were not difficult. I explained to her that, in fact, this was the very essence of my cooking style: I often combine a generous number of ingredients in order to build "layers of flavors" within a dish. It was then, as I was articulating my cooking philosophy, that the title for this cookbook – and its theme – were born.

Of course, recipes do not have to have lots of ingredients to be good. In fact, many of my recipes call for very few ingredients. My point is not to add ingredients indiscriminately – this would have the effect of masking flavors, not enhancing them. Instead, my purpose in *Layers of Flavors* is to help you learn to combine the unique tastes, textures, and aromas of various ingredients to create dishes that are more than the sum of their parts, dishes that are full-flavored, delicious, and uncomplicated.

A vital part of my effort to build layers of flavors is to use the freshest produce from the global kitchen. Cooking techniques and ingredients in *Layers of Flavors* combine influences from the Pacific Rim and the Mediterranean with the best of Californian, Southern, and other traditional

American fare to appeal to today's sophisticated tastes. Nowadays, so-called exotic ingredients are easy to find at your local grocery store or farmers market.

I have divided the recipes among five chapters: Starters, Entrees, Side Dishes, Breads, and Desserts. In my opinion, these divisions better reflect how we eat and entertain today than do more formal divisions, such as first course, second course, salads, etc. For instance, traditional menu planning might restrict a risotto to a first course, rather than a Side Dish, which is where I have it here. On the other hand, Thai-Style Noodles with Crunchy Vegetables, also a Side Dish in this book, would work equally well as an entree for many occasions. Whatever works in a menu is appropriate, in my philosophy.

Finally, let me repeat what I have told thousands of my students at my cooking school over the years: These recipes are simply blueprints – guidelines – to get you cooking. I expect you to adjust and adapt them to make them your own. You alone know what you, your family and your friends prefer. Above all remember: Relax, have fun, and begin to enjoy the confidence in the kitchen that this book aims to inspire in you.

STARTERS

Winter Root Vegetable Tart with Three Cheeses

Pecan-Smoked Trout Spread

Creamy Crab, Parmesan, and Chipotle Dip

Provençal Tapenade Croûtes

Arugula, Pine Nut, and Parmesan Salad

Classic Caesar Salad

Guiltless Caesar Salad

Mixed Baby Greens with Champagne Raspberry Vinaigrette

Blood Orange and Red Onion Salad with Feta Vinaigrette

Beautiful Bouquet Salad with Cilantro Lime Vinaigrette

Japanese Spinach Salad with Sesame Ginger Vinaigrette

Leek and Stilton Cheese Soufflé

Marbled Melon Soup

Roasted Garlic and Onion Soup with Fennel

Gingered Sweet Potato and Apple Vichyssoise

Sorrel Watercress Soup

WINTER ROOT VEGETABLE TART WITH THREE CHEESES

This versatile tart makes an elegant beginning to a dinner party or a delicious main course for a Sunday night supper.

SERVES 8

Basic Flaky Pie Crust dough (page 124)
1 small sweet potato, peeled and grated
1 small turnip, peeled and grated
1 cup grated Gruyère cheese
1 Vidalia onion, thinly sliced
2 garlic cloves, chopped
1 cup crumbled blue cheese
½ teaspoon salt
½ teaspoon black pepper
⅔ cup heavy cream
2 eggs, beaten lightly
1 cup freshly grated Parmesan cheese

Preheat the oven to 375°F. Roll out the pastry and place in a 10-inch tart tin with a removeable bottom. Prebake for 15 minutes and set aside to cool.

Arrange the grated sweet potato and turnip on the bottom of the tart crust. Top with grated Gruyère cheese. Layer the sliced Vidalia onion over the cheese and sprinkle with garlic. Top with crumbled blue cheese.

In a small bowl whisk together the salt, pepper, heavy cream, and beaten eggs. Carefully pour this over the tart. Bake for 20 minutes. Cover with Parmesan cheese and continue baking for 20 to 25 minutes, or until nicely browned.

Remove from the oven and place on a wire rack to cool. Remove the tart from the pan and place on a serving platter. Cut into wedges and serve slightly warm or at room temperature.

VARIATION Make this an onion tart by substituting a red onion and the white part of four chopped leeks for the sweet potato and turnip.

PECAN-SMOKED TROUT SPREAD

One of my students first introduced me to freshly smoked Georgia brook trout. She has a cabin in the North Georgia mountains, where a retired gentleman neighbor enjoys catching these fish and smoking them over cider-soaked pecan shells and applewood. Smoked trout is readily available in large supermarket delis and farmers markets. I usually serve this spread with crackers or French bread, but it is also very good spooned onto cucumber rounds or piped into hollowed-out cherry tomatoes.

MAKES 4 CUPS

1 pound smoked trout, deboned and skin removed
1 cup chopped pecans, lightly toasted*
2 (8 ounce) packages cream cheese, softened
1 cup sour cream
½ cup mayonnaise
¼ cup pepper-flavored vodka
¼ cup lemon juice
2 tablespoons Dijon mustard
2 tablespoons prepared horseradish
2 tablespoons chopped fresh dill
2 tablespoons capers, rinsed and drained
Freshly ground black pepper
4 green onions, chopped

To toast nuts, preheat the oven to 350°F. Spread the nuts on a baking sheet, place in the oven, and toast, stirring occasionally, for 6 to 8 minutes, or until golden brown.

Pick through the smoked trout for any small bones. Flake the fish.

In a food processor, combine half of the smoked trout with the toasted pecans, cream cheese, sour cream, mayonnaise, vodka, lemon juice, mustard, horseradish, dill, and capers. Process until smooth. Transfer the mixture to a medium bowl and fold in the remaining smoked trout. Season to taste with pepper and top with green onions.

Place the spread in a serving bowl or crock and surround with crackers or French bread.

MAKE AHEAD | This spread will keep in the refrigerator for 3 to 4 days before serving. It also freezes well for about 3 months. Thaw in the refrigerator. Stir well before serving, and top with the green onions.

CREAMY CRAB, PARMESAN, AND CHIPOTLE DIP

I love the unexpected flavor that chipotles impart to this dip. Chipotles, which are dried, smoked jalapeños, add a strong, spicy, smoky character. In larger supermarkets and specialty food stores you can often find canned chipotles with Mexican adobo sauce. If you buy chipotles loose, you will need to reconstitute them in water before using. Try stirring chipotles into mashed potatoes, risottos, or couscous. The added depth of flavor is phenomenal.

MAKES 4 CUPS

2 (8 ounce) containers pasteurized crabmeat, picked over
1 (10 ounce) package frozen chopped spinach, defrosted and squeezed dry
2 cups freshly grated Parmesan cheese, divided
1 onion, chopped
2 garlic cloves, chopped
1 (8 ounce) package cream cheese, softened
¼ cup mayonnaise
1 egg, lightly beaten
1 to 2 chipotles, soaked in water for 20 minutes and finely chopped, or 1 to 2 teaspoons
    chipotle in adobo sauce
Salt and freshly ground black pepper
2 teaspoons chili powder

Preheat the oven to 350°F.

In a large bowl mix together the crabmeat, spinach, 1½ cups of the Parmesan cheese, onion, garlic, cream cheese, mayonnaise, egg, chipotles, and salt and pepper to taste.

Lightly butter a 12-inch gratin dish or ovenproof casserole. Spoon the mixture into the prepared dish. In a small bowl mix together the reserved ½ cup of Parmesan cheese and chili powder. Sprinkle over the crab mixture.

Bake for 20 to 25 minutes, or until hot and bubbly. Serve warm with Lavash flatbread, pita wedges, tortilla chips, or crackers.

MAKE AHEAD The uncooked dip freezes well, tightly wrapped, for up to 2 months. Defrost overnight in the refrigerator before baking.

NOTE For a quick and easy finger hors d'oeuvre, spoon or pipe the dip onto cocktail bread rounds and run under the broiler for 1 to 2 minutes until hot and bubbling. The dip also holds well in a small chafing dish.

PROVENÇAL TAPENADE CROÛTES

You can serve this robust spread on croûtes, as we do here, or use it in salad dressings, tossed with cooked pasta or freshly steamed vegetables, stirred into soups or stews, mixed with sour cream as a dip for crudités, or stirred into mayonnaise as a spread for sandwiches.

MAKES 2 CUPS

2 cups rinsed and drained niçoise or Greek kalamata olives, halved and pitted
6 anchovy fillets packed in oil, drained
4 garlic cloves, finely chopped
3 green onions, chopped
3 tablespoons capers, rinsed and drained
1 tablespoon herbes de Provence or Italian seasoning mix
¼ cup chopped fresh basil
2 tablespoons chopped fresh parsley
⅓ cup extra-virgin olive oil
3 tablespoons lemon juice
Freshly ground black pepper
Very thinly sliced French bread, lightly toasted

In a food processor combine the olives, anchovies, garlic, green onions, capers, herbes de Provence or Italian seasoning mix, basil, and parsley. Process until the mixture is very finely chopped to almost a smooth puree.

With the machine running, gradually add the olive oil in a thin, steady stream until the mixture is very smooth and paste-like. Stir in the lemon juice and season to taste with pepper. Serve at room temperature, spread on lightly toasted French bread.

MAKE AHEAD | The tapenade keeps for about a week, tightly covered, in the refrigerator.

VARIATION | Add ½ cup oil-packed sun-dried tomatoes with the olives at the beginning of the recipe.

ARUGULA, PINE NUT, AND PARMESAN SALAD

For all its seeming simplicity, this salad is alive with tastes and textures. Ingredients should be the finest you can buy. This is the time to use your best vinegars and olive oil. You will truly taste the difference. This recipe has been adapted from Patricia Wells' *Trattoria*.

SERVES 8

2 cups stemmed arugula leaves, washed and dried
6 cups mesclun (sometimes called spring mix or California mix), washed and dried
1 cup basil leaves, washed and dried
1½ cups shaved Parmesan cheese, preferably Parmigiano-Reggiano
¾ cup pine nuts, lightly toasted (see page 7)
Kosher salt and freshly ground black pepper
1 tablespoon red wine vinegar
1 tablespoon balsamic vinegar
1 tablespoon sherry vinegar
2 tablespoons extra-virgin olive oil

In a large bowl mix together the arugula, mesclun, basil leaves, Parmesan cheese, pine nuts, and salt and pepper to taste.

Drizzle the greens with red wine vinegar, balsamic vinegar, and sherry vinegar. Toss to coat. Drizzle with extra-virgin olive oil and toss once more. The oil should just barely coat the greens. Serve at once.

NOTES To shave Parmesan, first bring the cheese to room temperature. Using a vegetable peeler, make long, even shavings from the block of cheese.

Remember the five degrees of doneness whenever you toast a nut:
1) almost done
2) almost done
3) almost done
4) almost done
5) BURNT!!!

CLASSIC CAESAR SALAD

You can top this all-time favorite with grilled shrimp, chicken, or broiled salmon to transform it into a main meal. The dressing makes a delicious dip for fresh crudités, or toss it with boiled and sliced new potatoes for a very different potato salad. If raw eggs are a concern, substitute ½ cup egg substitute.

SERVES | 8

4 garlic cloves, peeled
8 anchovy fillets packed in oil, drained
1 tablespoon capers, rinsed and drained
1 tablespoon Dijon mustard
4 egg yolks
⅓ cup red wine vinegar
1 tablespoon Worcestershire sauce
1 cup vegetable oil
2 heads Romaine lettuce, washed and separated into leaves or torn into bite-sized pieces
1 cup shaved Parmesan cheese
2 cups store-bought seasoned croutons
Salt and freshly ground black pepper
Parmesan Garlic Croûtes

In a food processor or blender combine the garlic cloves, anchovies, and capers until well blended, like a paste. Add the mustard, egg yolks, vinegar, and Worcestershire sauce. Blend until smooth. With the machine running, slowly pour in the vegetable oil until the dressing is thick and creamy. This process should take about 1½ to 2 minutes.

In a large serving bowl, toss the Romaine with the dressing, Parmesan cheese, croutons, and salt and pepper to taste. Serve at once, with Parmesan Garlic Croûtes, if desired.

PARMESAN GARLIC CROÛTES

8 to 10 slices of day-old French bread
¼ cup olive oil
2 garlic cloves, finely chopped
¼ cup freshly grated Parmesan cheese
½ teaspoon red pepper flakes

Preheat the broiler. Place the slices of French bread on a baking sheet. In a small bowl, whisk together the remaining ingredients. Brush each piece of bread with an equal amount of this mixture. Broil for 1 to 2 minutes, or until the bread is heated through and the edges just begin to brown. Serve with Classic Caesar Salad.

MAKE AHEAD | The dressing keeps in the refrigerator for 3 days. Store croutons in an airtight container for up to 3 days.

NOTE | To avoid raw eggs, gently heat the yokes in a double boiler over simmering water, continually whisking, until they reach a temperature of 160°F.

GUILTLESS CAESAR SALAD

I had to include this version of the classic salad because so many of my colleagues said a low-fat, good tasting Caesar salad couldn't be done. Well, here it is, and I dare say it's hard to tell the two apart.

SERVES | 8

3 garlic cloves, peeled
4 anchovy fillets
1 tablespoon capers, rinsed and drained
2 tablespoons Dijon mustard
½ cup egg substitute
⅓ cup red wine vinegar
1 tablespoon Worcestershire sauce
2 cups nonfat sour cream
2 heads romaine lettuce, washed and separated into leaves or torn into bite-sized pieces
1 cup fat-free shredded Parmesan cheese
Salt and freshly ground black pepper
Seasoned Fat-Free Croutons

In a food processor or blender combine the garlic cloves, anchovies, and capers until well blended, like a paste. Add the mustard, egg substitute, vinegar, and Worcestershire sauce. Blend until smooth. With the machine running, slowly add in the nonfat sour cream until dressing is thick and creamy.

In a large serving bowl, toss the Romaine with the dressing, Parmesan cheese, croutons, and salt and pepper to taste. Serve at once.

SEASONED FAT-FREE CROUTONS

4 to 6 slices of day-old French bread, cubed
Nonstick cooking spray
1 tablespoon dried Italian seasoning
½ teaspoon onion powder
½ teaspoon garlic powder
¼ teaspoon cayenne pepper

Preheat the oven to 350°F. Scatter the cubed bread on a large baking sheet. Spray lightly with nonstick cooking spray. Sprinkle with Italian seasoning, onion powder, garlic powder, and cayenne pepper. Toss to coat completely. Bake for 10 minutes, or until golden and crisp.

MAKE AHEAD | The dressing keeps in the refrigerator for 7 days. Store croutons in an airtight container for 1 week or freeze for 1 month.

MIXED BABY GREENS WITH CHAMPAGNE RASPBERRY VINAIGRETTE

Not only is this salad delicious, it is one of the prettiest you can serve, and one of my favorites. I like the contrast in taste between the bitter greens and the sweet raspberries, and the differing textures of the crisp radish slices and crunchy walnuts. This dressing is also wonderful in fresh fruit salad.

SERVES 8

½ cup dry champagne (can be flat) or dry white wine
⅓ cup red raspberry vinegar
1 tablespoon Dijon mustard
1 tablespoon sugar
½ teaspoon salt
½ teaspoon black pepper
1 tablespoon poppy seeds
½ cup extra-virgin olive oil
10 cups mixed baby greens, such as Bibb, Boston, red leaf, romaine, and radicchio,
    washed, dried, and torn into bite-sized pieces
1 cup sliced mushrooms
1 bunch radishes, stemmed, washed, and thinly sliced
1 cup walnut halves, lightly toasted (see page 7)
1 cup fresh raspberries

In a small bowl whisk together the champagne or wine, vinegar, mustard, sugar, salt, pepper, and poppy seeds. Add the olive oil in a thin, steady stream, whisking constantly until dressing is thick. Set aside.

In a large bowl toss together mixed greens, mushrooms, and radish slices. Pour half of the dressing on the salad and toss to coat. Sprinkle with the walnut halves and raspberries. Pass the remaining dressing separately, or drizzle remaining dressing on the salad after it has been topped with the walnuts and raspberries. Serve at once.

BLOOD ORANGE AND RED ONION SALAD WITH FETA VINAIGRETTE

The feta and oregano in the vinaigrette give this salad a distinctly Greek flavor. The salad complements any pasta dish and is especially nice with Asian Barbecued Turkey Breast.

SERVES 8

1 (10 ounce) package prewashed spinach, stems removed
1 large red onion, peeled and thinly sliced into rings
4 blood or navel oranges, peeled and thinly sliced crosswise (see note page 140)
1 cup thinly sliced radishes
½ cup pitted Greek black olives
⅓ cup apple cider vinegar
2 tablespoons Dijon mustard
2 tablespoons chopped fresh oregano
3 garlic cloves, chopped
¼ cup capers, rinsed and drained
½ teaspoon salt
½ teaspoon black pepper
2 teaspoons sugar
½ cup extra-virgin olive oil
1 cup crumbled feta cheese

On a large serving platter layer the spinach, red onion, oranges, radishes, and black olives. In a small bowl combine the apple cider vinegar, mustard, oregano, garlic, capers, salt, pepper, and sugar. Slowly whisk in the olive oil in a thin, steady stream. Mix in the feta cheese and stir to combine. Pour vinaigrette over the salad. Serve at once.

BEAUTIFUL BOUQUET SALAD
WITH CILANTRO LIME VINAIGRETTE

This salad looks like a beautiful flower arrangement on a plate. Edible flowers will enhance the effect. I adapted this recipe from one featured on the PBS television program, *Cooking at the Academy*.

SERVES | 8

¼ cup chopped fresh cilantro
1 garlic clove, chopped
¼ cup freshly squeezed lime juice
2 tablespoons sugar
½ cup extra-virgin olive oil
Salt and freshly ground black pepper
8 large tomatoes
2 small heads red oak (not red leaf) lettuce, washed and dried
1 head frisée or curly endive, washed and dried
1 small head radicchio, washed and dried
2 Belgian endives, washed, dried, tough core removed, and separated into spears
1 small bunch enoki mushrooms, washed and dried
Whole chives
Edible flowers, such as nasturtiums or marigolds

Make the vinaigrette: In a medium bowl combine the cilantro, garlic, lime juice, and sugar. Slowly whisk in the olive oil in a steady stream. Season to taste with salt and pepper. Set aside.

Cut thin slices from the top and bottom of each tomato. With a small spoon or melon baller, remove the pulp and discard. Twist or cut off the ends of the lettuces. Arrange 5 or 6 red oak lettuce leaves on top of each other, fanning them slightly. Stack a few of the frisée leaves, radicchio leaves, and endive leaves on top of the red oak. Carefully roll up, jelly-roll fashion, and place one end in the tomato cup, arranging the leaves as you would flowers to create a bouquet effect. Repeat with remaining lettuce and tomatoes. Insert a few enoki mushrooms, fresh whole chives, and edible flowers into each tomato and arrange decoratively. Place on individual serving plates or one large platter.

Pass the vinaigrette separately or drizzle around each individual bouquet just before serving.

JAPANESE SPINACH SALAD WITH SESAME GINGER VINAIGRETTE

The dressing in this salad also makes a good marinade for chicken, pork, or fish. Wasabi, or Japanese horseradish, is available in dry or paste forms. You can substitute dry mustard if wasabi is unavailable.

SERVES 8

¼ cup rice wine vinegar

¼ cup dry sherry

¼ cup soy sauce

3 tablespoons dark Asian sesame oil

¼ cup peanut oil

2 tablespoons sugar

2 to 3 teaspoons wasabi powder

3 garlic cloves, chopped

2 tablespoons chopped fresh ginger

¼ cup lightly toasted sesame seeds (see page 7)

1 (10 ounce) package prewashed spinach leaves, stems removed

1 head radicchio, washed, dried, and thinly sliced

3 Belgian endives, washed, dried, tough core removed, and separated into spears

1 cup bean sprouts, rinsed and drained

1 (8 ounce) can sliced water chestnuts, rinsed and drained

2 bunches enoki mushrooms, rinsed and drained

1 cucumber, halved lengthwise, seeded, and thinly sliced into crescents

½ cup chopped fresh cilantro

Make the vinaigrette: In a medium bowl or a small jar with a tight-fitting lid, combine the rice wine vinegar, dry sherry, soy sauce, sesame oil, peanut oil, sugar, wasabi powder, garlic, ginger, and sesame seeds. Whisk or shake until well blended. Chill for 1 hour, stirring briefly to incorporate ingredients just before serving.

In a large bowl toss together the spinach leaves, radicchio, endive, bean sprouts, water chestnuts, mushrooms, cucumber, and cilantro. Toss well. Drizzle half of the vinaigrette over the greens and pass the remaining dressing separately.

MAKE AHEAD | The dressing will keep for up to 2 weeks in the refrigerator.

NOTE | I never peel my ginger root. I wash it very well and then chop or grate it, peel and all, for use in recipes. I store leftover pieces of ginger immersed in dry sherry in a glass jar in the refrigerator. Not only does this preserve the fresh ginger, it imparts a wonderful flavor to the dry sherry. Use this ginger-infused sherry to perk up marinades, salad dressings, and stir fries. A couple of tablespoons in a flute topped off with champagne makes a delightful, refreshing aperitif.

LEEK AND STILTON CHEESE SOUFFLÉ

There's a very true culinary saying: "Everyone will wait for a good soufflé, but a good soufflé waits for no one." When serving a soufflé, timing is indeed everything. Fortunately, you can make the base of the soufflé up to a day ahead. Then all you need to do at the last minute is beat the egg whites, fold them into the base, and bake.

SERVES | 4 TO 6

½ cup finely grated Parmesan cheese
4 tablespoons butter
6 leeks, white part only, cleaned and thinly sliced
3 tablespoons flour
1½ cups half and half
4 ounces Stilton cheese, crumbled (about 1 cup)
Freshly grated nutmeg
Salt and freshly ground black pepper
6 eggs, separated

Preheat the oven to 400°F. Lightly butter the inside of an 8-cup soufflé dish. Sprinkle the Parmesan cheese in the dish and roll it around evenly, coating the sides and bottom of the dish. Set aside.

In a 2-quart saucepan over medium heat, melt the butter and add the leeks. Cook for 5 minutes, or until the leeks are softened. Stir in the flour and cook, stirring constantly, until the mixture becomes straw colored, about 2 or 3 minutes. Stir in the half and half and whisk until smooth and thick.

Remove from the heat and add the Stilton, stirring until just melted. Add the nutmeg and season to taste with salt and pepper. Let the mixture cool for 5 minutes. Quickly stir in the egg yolks and set aside, keeping mixture warm.

In a clean bowl, preferably copper, beat the egg whites until stiff peaks form. Fold ¼ of the egg whites into the cheese mixture, then fold the lightened cheese mixture gently into the remaining egg whites. Pour the mixture into the prepared soufflé dish and place on a baking sheet in the upper half of the oven. Immediately reduce the heat to 350°F and bake the soufflé until lightly browned and puffy, and a skewer inserted into the center comes out clean but moist. This will take 25 to 30 minutes. Serve at once.

NOTES | Egg whites beaten in a dry copper bowl will hold their shape for 15 to 20 minutes longer than those beaten in another type of bowl and produce a finished soufflé about twice as high in volume. The copper acts as a stabilizer for the egg whites. (To remove tarnish from a copper bowl, combine 1 tablespoon salt and 1 tablespoon distilled vinegar. Using a paper towel, wipe bowl with this mixture, then rinse thoroughly and dry. The salt acts as an abrasive and the vinegar as a mild acid to remove the tarnish.) If you do not have a copper bowl, use a stainless steel bowl and add a pinch of cream of tartar to the egg whites. Always make sure there is not a single speck of yolk in the whites. Any yolk will inhibit the whites from absorbing air and beating to their fullest volume. Never beat egg whites in a plastic bowl. Plastic is porous and will sometimes hold traces of fat, which can prevent egg whites from beating to their proper volume.

Eggs will separate more easily when they are chilled, but the whites will beat to their highest volume when they are at room temperature.

MARBLED MELON SOUP

This totally fat-free soup makes a cooling first course on a hot summer night, or a refreshing light dessert after a spring feast. I also like to serve it at casual Sunday brunches. If you like, drizzle a splash of Midori (melon liqueur) over the individual bowls just before serving.

SERVES | 8

1 large cantaloupe, seeded, peeled, and coarsely chopped
3 ripe peaches, peeled, pitted, and sliced
Juice of 1 lemon
½ teaspoon ground coriander
½ cup honey, divided
1 medium-sized honeydew melon, seeded, peeled, and coarsely chopped
3 kiwi fruit, peeled and sliced
Juice of 2 limes
1 tablespoon chopped fresh mint, plus additional for garnish
Assorted fruits and berries (peaches, melon balls, kiwi, starfruit, strawberries, blueberries, and raspberries)

In a food processor puree the cantaloupe, sliced peaches, lemon juice, coriander, and ¼ cup of honey until smooth. Pour into a medium bowl, cover, and refrigerate.

Rinse the bowl and blade of the machine thoroughly. Puree the honeydew, kiwi fruit, lime juice, mint, and remaining honey until smooth. Pour into another medium bowl, cover, and refrigerate.

For best flavor, chill the fruit purees for 6 hours or overnight. At serving time, ladle ½ cup of each puree into individual soup bowls, allowing the colors to mix in the middle. To create a swirled or marbled pattern, draw a knife tip or thin spatula through the surface of the purees.

Garnish with additional chopped mint and fruit of your choice. I like to place different fruits and berries in small bowls and let my guests top their soup as desired. Serve at once.

NOTE | If serving this for dessert, top with toasted pound cake croutons: Slice 4 pieces of Perfect Butter Pound Cake (page 145). Cut slices into ¾-inch cubes and toast in a preheated 400°F oven for 8 to 10 minutes, or until golden brown. Sprinkle on the soup just before serving, or let guests top their soup as desired.

ROASTED GARLIC AND ONION SOUP WITH FENNEL

The garlic and onions in this soup develop a very sweet, mellow flavor as they slowly caramelize in the oven. For the flavor to develop to the fullest, let the mixture become a rich pecan brown.

SERVES 8

2 heads garlic, separated into cloves and peeled (about 24 cloves)
4 onions, sliced
2 fennel bulbs, thinly sliced (reserve the fronds)
⅓ cup olive oil
½ teaspoon salt
½ teaspoon black pepper
1 tablespoon flour
9 cups beef stock
1 cup grated Gruyère cheese

Preheat the oven to 375°F. In a large ovenproof baking dish, toss the garlic, onion, and fennel slices with the olive oil. Sprinkle this mixture with the salt, pepper, and flour.

Place in the oven and bake for 1½ hours, or until vegetables are soft, tender, and a rich golden brown color. Stir the mixture every 15 minutes or so to promote even browning.

In a 4½-quart Dutch oven, bring the beef stock to a boil. Add the caramelized vegetables. Reduce the heat to a simmer and cook for 10 minutes. Remove the solids to a food processor or blender and puree until smooth. Return this mixture to the stock and blend thoroughly. Taste for seasonings and add salt and pepper as needed.

Ladle the hot soup into individual bowls and top each with Gruyère cheese. Chop the reserved fennel fronds and sprinkle over the soup. Serve at once.

NOTE For a more rustic soup, do not puree the solids. Gently mash them with the back of a spoon or a potato masher.

GINGERED SWEET POTATO AND APPLE VICHYSSOISE

I adapted this special potato soup from Lee Bailey's *Soup Meals*. Keep in mind that chilled dishes need more seasonings — especially salt and pepper — than hot dishes.

SERVES 8

4 sweet potatoes
2 tablespoons finely chopped candied ginger
3 leeks, white part only, cleaned and thinly sliced
6 green onions, thinly sliced
3 Golden Delicious apples, peeled, cored, and sliced
3 cups chicken stock
Grated zest of 1 lemon
Salt and freshly ground black pepper
3 cups apple cider
1 cup heavy cream
2 tablespoons chopped chives
⅓ cup chopped pecans or walnuts, lightly toasted (see page 7)

Preheat the oven to 400°F. Scrub the sweet potatoes, pierce each one several times with a fork, and place in the oven on a baking sheet. Bake until soft, about 1 hour.

Meanwhile, in a 4½-quart Dutch oven, combine the candied ginger, leeks, green onions, apple slices, chicken stock, lemon zest, and salt and pepper to taste. Bring to a boil, reduce the heat to a simmer, and cook, covered, for 15 to 20 minutes, or until the leeks are very tender.

Split the sweet potatoes in half and scoop out the pulp. Add the sweet potato pulp to the hot stock and simmer 5 minutes.

Place this mixture, in batches if necessary, into a food processor or blender and puree until smooth. Return the pureed mixture to the Dutch oven and stir in the apple cider. Adjust to taste with additional salt and pepper. Cover and chill until ready to serve, at least 4 hours.

When ready to serve, lightly whip the cream to a mousse-like consistency. Stir cream into soup and top with chopped chives and nuts. Serve at once.

NOTE This soup is also delicious served hot. You can make it ahead and reheat it, stirring in the cream just before serving. A drizzle of Calvados or Applejack heightens the apple flavor in the hot soup.

SORREL WATERCRESS SOUP

The peppery bite of watercress combines with the lemony zing of sorrel leaves to produce a soup that will stimulate appetites.

SERVES | 8

½ pound asparagus, washed, tough ends removed
4 tablespoons butter
¼ cup chopped fresh sorrel or parsley
1 red onion, chopped
1 leek (white and light green part only), washed and coarsely chopped
2 ribs of celery, chopped
1 baking potato, peeled and cubed
2 bunches watercress (leaves and tender stems only), rinsed and dried
8 cups chicken stock
1 tablespoon lemon juice
Salt and white pepper
1 cup heavy cream

GARNISHES

About 12 sorrel leaves
Sour cream
About ¼ pound slivered prosciutto

Snap off the asparagus tips and set the stalks aside. In a large sauté pan melt the butter over medium heat, add the chopped sorrel or parsley, and cook for 30 seconds. Add the asparagus tips, red onion, leek, celery, potato, and watercress leaves. Cover tightly and cook over very low heat until the vegetables are soft, about 25 to 30 minutes.

Meanwhile, place the chicken stock in a large saucepan with the reserved asparagus stalks. Bring to a boil, reduce heat, and simmer, covered, for about 30 minutes. Discard the asparagus stalks.

In a food processor, puree the softened vegetables with a little bit of the stock to make a smooth, silky mixture. Stir the pureed vegetables into the remaining stock, and season with lemon juice and salt and white pepper to taste. Stir in cream and bring soup to just below a simmer.

Create a chiffonade of sorrel: Layer sorrel leaves on top of each other and roll up like a cigar. Slice very thinly. Separate the leaves into individual strips. Ladle soup into individual bowls and garnish each serving with a dollop of sour cream, chiffonade of sorrel, and slivers of prosciutto.

NOTE This soup is also good chilled. Add garnishes just before serving.

ENTREES

Moroccan Lemon Chicken

Turkey Piccata

Baked Chicken with Mustard Glaze

Balsamic Roasted Chicken with Garlic and Fresh Herbs

Szechwan Chicken and Shrimp Brochettes

Asian Barbecued Turkey Breast with Fiery Harissa Sauce

Garlic Pan-Roasted Shrimp

Sizzling Spring Ginger Salmon

Classic Cod Cakes with Jalapeño Tartar Sauce

Blue Cornmeal Catfish Fillets with Toasted Pecan Butter

Succulent Seafood Jambalaya

Lemon-Marinated Leg of Lamb with Mint Gremolata

Molasses- and Cider-Basted Loin of Pork

Southwestern Apple and Red Chile Chutney

Apple Serrano Salsa

Tri-Mustard Pork

Zesty Black Bean Salsa

Herb-Crusted Beef Tenderloin with Sunshine Béarnaise Sauce

Ratatouille Gratin

Versatile Vegetable Sauce

Penne Baked with Exotic Mushrooms

Phyllo-Layered Vegetable Strudel

MOROCCAN LEMON CHICKEN

This fragrant chicken is alive with vibrant flavors and textures. A simple dish of couscous and a loaf of crusty bread complete this meal.

SERVES 8

1 yellow onion, chopped
6 garlic cloves, chopped
1 teaspoon turmeric
1 tablespoon ground cumin
1 teaspoon red pepper flakes
¼ cup chopped fresh cilantro
¼ cup chopped fresh parsley
¼ cup olive oil
Grated zest and juice of 3 lemons
8 boneless, skinless chicken breasts
2 red onions, thinly sliced
1 (10 ounce) package prewashed spinach, stems removed
4 tomatoes, seeded and cut into 1-inch cubes
½ teaspoon salt
½ teaspoon black pepper
8 thin slices of lemon
½ cup sliced almonds
½ cup currants
4 green onions, chopped

In a food processor, make a paste by combining the yellow onion, garlic, turmeric, ground cumin, red pepper flakes, cilantro, parsley, olive oil, and lemon zest and juice. Rub mixture liberally over the chicken breasts. Cover and refrigerate for 2 hours or overnight.

Preheat the oven to 400°F. In a large bowl, toss together the red onions, spinach, and tomatoes. Place in a lightly oiled 13 x 9 x 2-inch baking pan. Remove the chicken from the refrigerator and place on top of the vegetables, covering with any additional marinade. Sprinkle the chicken and vegetables with salt and pepper. Top each chicken breast with a slice of lemon and sprinkle with sliced almonds and currants.

Cover with aluminum foil and bake for 20 minutes. Remove the foil and bake for an additional 20 minutes. Sprinkle with green onions just before serving. Serve in the baking dish or on a serving platter, with the chicken breasts on top of the vegetables.

TURKEY PICCATA

The term *piccata* indicates a piquancy or an aromatic, sharp flavor. That certainly describes this bright, full-flavored dish. One of my favorite entrees to serve to hungry guests, Turkey Piccata is wonderful paired with a simple salad and a zesty risotto. You can substitute veal for the less expensive turkey cutlets, but it is difficult to tell the difference between the two in the finished dish.

SERVES | 8

8 boneless turkey breast cutlets
⅔ cup all-purpose flour
2 tablespoons cornstarch
1 tablespoon chopped fresh rosemary
1 tablespoon chopped fresh oregano
¼ teaspoon cayenne pepper
½ teaspoon salt
3 tablespoons butter
3 tablespoons olive oil

½ cup dry sherry
⅓ cup lemon juice
½ cup chicken stock
¼ cup capers, rinsed and drained
4 green onions, chopped
2 garlic cloves, chopped
Salt and freshly ground black pepper
Lemon slices

Trim the cutlets of any visible fat. Place between two sheets of plastic wrap and pound the meat until it is about ¼-inch thick.

In a shallow bowl or pie plate, combine the flour, cornstarch, rosemary, oregano, cayenne pepper, and salt. Dredge the meat on both sides in the mixture. Set aside.

Heat a large sauté pan over medium heat until hot. Add the butter and olive oil, swirling the pan to coat completely. Add the meat and cook for 3 minutes on each side, or until browned. Remove the meat from the sauté pan and drain on paper towels. Place on a heatproof serving platter, cover with foil, and place in a 200°F oven to keep warm.

Add the sherry, lemon juice, chicken stock, capers, green onions, and garlic to the sauté pan. Stir very well to loosen the browned bits in the bottom of the skillet. Cook over medium heat, stirring occasionally, until the sauce is thick and reduced by half, about 5 minutes. Season to taste with salt and pepper. Pour the sauce over the sautéed cutlets and garnish with lemon slices. Serve at once.

BAKED CHICKEN WITH MUSTARD GLAZE

I love to make this quick and easy main course for simple dinner parties with friends.

SERVES | 6

3 tablespoons mustard seeds
¼ cup apple cider vinegar
⅓ cup coarse-grained mustard
3 tablespoons lemon juice
¾ cup mayonnaise (can be reduced fat)
3 small shallots, finely chopped

2 tablespoons chopped fresh basil or 1
   tablespoon Italian Seasoning mix
Salt and freshly ground black pepper
6 boneless, skinless chicken breasts
½ cup seasoned bread crumbs
½ cup freshly grated Parmesan cheese

Preheat the oven to 400°F. Lightly butter a 14-inch gratin dish.

In a medium bowl combine mustard seeds and apple cider vinegar. Soak for 1 hour. This will soften the seeds for the glaze.

Add the mustard, lemon juice, mayonnaise, shallots, basil, and salt and pepper to taste. Spread about ⅓ of the mustard glaze on the bottom of the prepared gratin dish. Arrange the chicken breasts on top. Spoon and evenly spread the remaining glaze over the chicken. Sprinkle with bread crumbs and Parmesan cheese.

Bake for 25 to 30 minutes, or until the chicken is cooked all the way through and the glaze has just begun to brown. To facilitate browning, you can place the dish under the broiler for about 30 seconds to 1 minute. Serve at once.

MAKE AHEAD | You can prepare the chicken and glaze the night before serving and store, tightly covered, in the refrigerator. When ready to serve, uncover the chicken and place in the preheated oven. Add about 5 minutes of cooking time to compensate for the refrigeration.

VARIATION | Substitute 6 (6 ounce) tuna or swordfish steaks for the chicken. Omit the basil and Parmesan cheese. Add 3 tablespoons of freshly chopped dill and 1 tablespoon capers to the mustard glaze. Bake at 400°F for 15 to 20 minutes, or until the fish flakes easily with a fork. Note that the fish cannot be prepared ahead and kept in the refrigerator, as the acid from the vinegar and lemon juice would begin to "cook" the fish.

BALSAMIC ROASTED CHICKEN WITH GARLIC AND FRESH HERBS

A whole roast chicken is one of the simplest but most beloved main courses I know. When whole cloves of garlic are roasted they develop a very mellow, almost nut-like taste. This recipe is an adaptation of the James Beard classic.

SERVES | 4 TO 6

3 tablespoons olive oil
3 tablespoons butter
5 heads garlic, separated into cloves and peeled (about 60 cloves)
1 onion, peeled and quartered
1 cup chopped assorted fresh herbs, such as parsley, rosemary, tarragon, oregano, and basil
1 (5 pound) roasting chicken
2 cups chicken stock, divided
1 cup balsamic vinegar
½ cup red wine
3 tablespoons honey
Salt and freshly ground black pepper

Preheat the oven to 425°F. In a skillet heat the oil and butter over medium heat. Add the garlic cloves and onion and sauté until lightly browned, about 15 minutes. Stir in half of the chopped herbs. Remove the garlic and the onions with a slotted spoon, leaving the excess oil in the pan, and place them in the cavity of the bird. Brush the chicken with the reserved pan drippings.

Place the chicken in a roasting pan. With kitchen twine, tie or truss the legs together. Add 1 cup of the chicken stock to the roasting pan. Bake for 1 hour. Remove from the oven, baste the bird, add the remaining cup of stock, and bake for 1 hour longer, or until the internal temperature reaches 180 degrees.

Remove the chicken and allow to sit. To the roasting pan add the balsamic vinegar, red wine, and honey. Remove the garlic mixture from the chicken and add to the pan. Bring to a boil and boil steadily until the liquid is reduced by about half. Skim off any fat, stir in the remaining herbs and season to taste with salt and pepper. Cut the chicken into 8 pieces and arrange on a serving platter. Ladle some of the reduced herb and garlic sauce over the chicken and pass the remaining sauce separately. For a smoother sauce, puree it in a food processor or blender.

NOTES Garlic is easy to peel when heated in the microwave. Place about 6 cloves at a time in the microwave and heat on full power for about 20 seconds. Carefully remove the garlic from the microwave. The skin should easily slip away from the cloves.

Unwaxed (and unflavored) dental floss can be used to truss the bird if kitchen twine is unavailable.

SZECHWAN CHICKEN AND SHRIMP BROCHETTES

These unusual brochettes make a pretty presentation at an elegant dinner party. I like to serve them with Thai-Style Noodles with Crunchy Vegetables or Pan-Roasted Barley Pilaf.

SERVES | 6

4 boneless, skinless chicken fillets
1 pound large shrimp
½ cup soy sauce
¼ cup dry sherry
Juice and grated zest of 1 orange
Juice and grated zest of 1 lime
⅓ cup orange blossom honey
3 tablespoons dark Asian sesame oil
2 tablespoons chopped ginger

3 green onions, chopped
3 garlic cloves, finely chopped
1 teaspoon crushed Szechwan or black peppercorns
2 small red onions, cut into sixths
2 medium zucchini, cut into 1-inch-thick rounds
2 red peppers, seeded and cut into 1½-inch pieces
12 metal or wooden skewers

If you are using wooden skewers, soak them in water for 1 hour before grilling or broiling. Cut the chicken into 1½-inch chunks and place in a medium bowl. Peel and devein the shrimp and place in another medium bowl.

In a large bowl whisk together the soy sauce, sherry, orange juice and zest, lime juice and zest, honey, sesame oil, ginger, green onions, garlic, and crushed peppercorns. Pour half of the marinade over the chicken and the other half over the shrimp. Toss to coat. Marinate in the refrigerator for 1 hour.

Preheat a broiler or prepare a medium-hot charcoal grill. On 6 skewers, alternately thread chicken cubes and vegetables. Alternate shrimp and vegetables on the remaining skewers. Place the brochettes about 6 inches from the heat source. Broil or grill the chicken brochettes for about 10 minutes per side and the shrimp for about 3 minutes per side (it should just begin to curl and turn pink), brushing with the remaining marinade as you turn the skewers. The vegetables on the shrimp brochettes will be crispier than those on the chicken brochettes.

ASIAN BARBECUED TURKEY BREAST WITH FIERY HARISSA SAUCE

This turkey breast is simmered first, then marinated, which allows the meat to develop a tremendous amount of flavor. The skin will crisp and glaze from the sugars in the marinade, but the meat underneath will remain moist and flavorful. Harissa is a fiery hot staple used as a flavoring in many Northern African dishes, especially couscous. Apple Serrano Salsa makes a fresh, lively accompaniment.

SERVES | 8 TO 10

1 (5 to 6 pound) turkey breast
1 onion, halved
4 garlic cloves
1 sprig of rosemary
1 sprig of thyme
1 sprig of parsley
3 whole cloves
10 black peppercorns
1 cup peach preserves
⅓ cup hot Chinese or Dijon mustard
¼ cup soy sauce
½ cup hoisin sauce
2 tablespoons dark Asian sesame oil
1 (12 ounce) can ginger ale
1 teaspoon red pepper flakes (optional)
4 garlic cloves, chopped
2 tablespoons chopped ginger
¼ cup chopped fresh lemongrass
4 green onions, chopped
Fiery Harissa Sauce

Place the turkey breast, onion, whole garlic cloves, rosemary, thyme, parsley, cloves, and black peppercorns in a large stockpot and cover with water by 2 inches. Bring to a boil, reduce the heat to a simmer, cover the pot, and cook the breast for about 1 hour. Remove the meat to a shallow dish and set aside. Reserve the stock for another use.

Meanwhile, in a large bowl whisk together peach preserves, mustard, soy sauce, hoisin sauce, sesame oil, ginger ale, red pepper flakes, chopped garlic, ginger, lemongrass, and green onions. Pour over the meat and marinate, covered, in the refrigerator, for at least 3 hours or overnight.

Preheat the oven to 400°F. Remove the turkey breast from the marinade and place in a large roasting pan. Roast until turkey is glazed and charred around the edges, about 30 to 40 minutes, basting with the reserved marinade as needed.

Thinly slice the breast meat and arrange on a serving platter. Pass the Harissa Sauce separately.

FIERY HARISSA SAUCE

10 dried hot chiles, stems removed
2 tablespoons cumin seeds
2 tablespoons coriander seeds
1 tablespoon yellow mustard seeds
2 teaspoons caraway seeds
6 garlic cloves, chopped
½ cup packed cilantro leaves
⅓ cup olive oil
Salt and freshly ground black pepper

In a small skillet break the dried chiles in half and add the cumin, coriander seed, mustard, and caraway seeds. Toast over medium-high heat, stirring constantly, until chiles and seeds just begin to smoke and are very fragrant, about 1 to 2 minutes. Transfer to a mini food processor and grind until coarse. Add the garlic and cilantro.

With the motor running, slowly pour in the olive oil and process until the mixture is a thick paste. Season to taste with salt and pepper. Refrigerate unused portion for up to 7 days. Use sparingly as a condiment for Asian Barbecued Turkey Breast. You can also stir it into couscous or risotto, or into sour cream as a dip for fresh crudités. This recipe makes about ¾ cup.

MAKE AHEAD | This dish can be made up to 24 hours before it is served. Store in the refrigerator, then slice the meat and allow to come to room temperature before serving.

NOTE | To prepare lemongrass, cut off the base of the bulb and trim away the dried outer leaves. Use the bottom 2 inches of the lemongrass. Coarsely chop the lemongrass, then pound slightly with the broad side of a knife to release the essential citronella oils.

GARLIC PAN-ROASTED SHRIMP

I always serve this delectable dish with a good Italian or French loaf to dip into the wonderful garlicky sauce. The shrimp and sauce can also be tossed with hot pasta or combined with White Beans with Tarragon and Niçoise Olives. A leafy green salad completes the meal. This dish makes good cocktail party fare; provide toothpicks for skewering the shrimp.

SERVES 6

2 pounds large shrimp, peeled and deveined
Salt and freshly ground black pepper
½ cup olive oil
6 garlic cloves, chopped
½ to 1 teaspoon red pepper flakes
¼ cup white wine or vermouth
2 tablespoons chopped fresh parsley
4 plum tomatoes, seeded and coarsely chopped

Spread the shrimp on a paper towel and blot dry with another towel. Season to taste with salt and pepper. Set aside.

In a large sauté pan heat the oil over medium heat until hot. Add the garlic and red pepper flakes and cook, stirring constantly, for 1 minute. Add the shrimp and briefly sauté, tossing the shrimp, until they begin to curl and turn pink, about 3 or 4 minutes. Add the wine or vermouth, cover, and allow the shrimp to steam for 30 seconds. Quickly transfer to a warmed serving platter and sprinkle with parsley and tomatoes. Season to taste with salt and pepper.

NOTE Be sure not to overcook the shrimp, as they will become tough and rubbery. A perfectly cooked shrimp should be a vibrant coral pink and form the letter C. If the tail curls too much and almost touches the other end, it has been overcooked.

SIZZLING SPRING GINGER SALMON

I love to hear the sizzling oil and smell its fragrant aroma when I drizzle it over the steamed salmon. If your wok does not have a steamer insert, use a round wire cooling rack or two chopsticks laid side by side.

SERVES | 4

4 (6 ounce) salmon fillets
4 green onions, trimmed and cut into 1-inch pieces (use the whole onion)
4 slices fresh ginger, cut into julienne strips
2 tablespoons dry sherry
2 tablespoons soy sauce
2 tablespoons peanut oil
2 green onions, finely chopped
1 tablespoon dark Asian sesame oil
1 tablespoon sesame seeds

Fill a large wok with enough water to almost reach the bottom of a steamer rack. Bring to a boil.

On a heatproof plate, arrange the salmon fillets in a single layer. Top with the 1-inch green onion pieces, ginger, dry sherry, and soy sauce. Place the plate on the steamer rack, cover the wok, and steam the fish for 6 to 8 minutes, or until the salmon is a pale pink and flakes easily with a fork.

Meanwhile, in a small skillet, heat the peanut oil and the finely chopped green onions to a sizzle. Stir in the dark Asian sesame oil and the sesame seeds. Drizzle immediately over the steamed salmon. Serve at once.

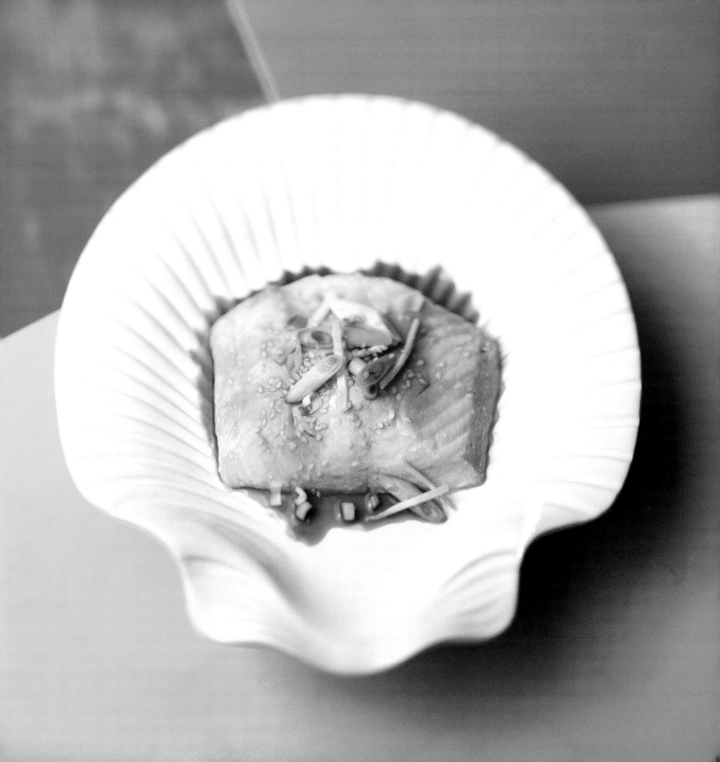

CLASSIC COD CAKES WITH JALAPEÑO TARTAR SAUCE

I first had these cod cakes at a small seaside restaurant in East Hampton, New York. I actually like them better than the more traditional crab cakes.

MAKES 12 CAKES, SERVING 6

1 pound salt cod, soaked in water overnight, rinsed, and drained
2 cups milk, divided
3 cups water
1 bay leaf
2 sprigs of thyme
4 sprigs of parsley
1 pound fresh boneless cod fillets
4 tablespoons butter
1 rib of celery, chopped
1 yellow onion, chopped
4 green onions, chopped
⅓ cup chopped fresh parsley
½ teaspoon Tabasco
1 tablespoon dry mustard
2 tablespoons Worcestershire sauce
¾ cup mayonnaise
2 eggs
Juice of 1 lemon
2½ cups seasoned bread crumbs, divided
Salt and freshly ground black pepper
2 egg yolks
½ cup cornmeal (not cornmeal mix)
¼ cup all-purpose flour
Fresh lemon wedges
Jalapeño Tartar Sauce

In a large saucepan mix together the soaked and drained salt cod, 1 cup of the milk, water, bay leaf, thyme, and parsley. Bring to a boil, reduce the heat to low, and cook for 15 minutes. Add the fresh cod and cook for 5 minutes. Drain and remove the fish to a large bowl to cool, discarding the flavoring ingredients. Flake fish with a fork and set aside.

In a large skillet melt the butter until sizzling. Add the celery and yellow onion and cook until the onion is translucent, about 5 minutes. Add the sautéed celery and onion to the flaked fish. Stir in the green onions, parsley, Tabasco, dry mustard, Worcestershire sauce, mayonnaise, eggs, lemon juice, 1½ cups of the bread crumbs, and salt and pepper to taste. Form the mixture into 12 cakes. Place on a baking sheet, cover, and refrigerate for 1 hour.

Preheat the oven to 375°F. In a small bowl whisk together the egg yolks and the remaining cup of milk. In a separate shallow pie plate combine the remaining cup of bread crumbs, cornmeal, and flour.

Dip cod cakes into the egg-and-milk mixture and dredge them in the bread crumb and cornmeal mixture.

Place the cod cakes on a baking sheet, with about 1 inch of space between them, and bake for 20 to 22 minutes, turning once, or until crispy and golden on the outside. Serve warm with fresh lemon wedges and Jalapeño Tartar Sauce.

JALAPEÑO TARTAR SAUCE

This zesty sauce can also be used as a spread for turkey or chicken sandwiches. For a smoky taste, substitute 2 teaspoons chipotle peppers in adobo sauce for the jalapeño.

2 egg yolks, very well chilled, or ¼ cup egg substitute
1 tablespoon Dijon mustard
½ cup olive oil
½ cup peanut oil
Juice of 1 lemon
Salt and freshly ground black pepper
1 dill pickle, finely chopped
1 jalapeño pepper, seeded and finely chopped

In a food processor or blender combine the egg yolks and mustard until well blended. With the machine running, slowly pour in the olive oil and the peanut oil simultaneously in thin, steady streams. Process until the mixture is thick and emulsified. This will take about 2 minutes. Quickly blend in the lemon juice, salt and pepper to taste, dill pickle, and chopped jalapeño pepper. Serve at once with Classic Cod Cakes. Makes about 1¼ cups.

MAKE AHEAD | The sauce can be refrigerated for up to 2 days.

NOTE | This makes an excellent addition to an hors d'oeuvre buffet when shaped into 36 one-inch cakes. Also, since they are baked and not fried, the cod cakes can be assembled ahead and "popped" in the oven at the last minute.

BLUE CORNMEAL CATFISH FILLETS WITH TOASTED PECAN BUTTER

Be sure to dollop the flavorful butter over the crispy fillets while they are piping hot to allow it to melt and flavor the fish. Blue cornmeal is widely available now in the international section of most grocery stores, but you can substitute yellow cornmeal.

SERVES | 8

8 (6 ounce) catfish fillets
1 cup buttermilk
2 eggs
1 teaspoon Tabasco
2 cups blue (or yellow) cornmeal
3 tablespoons chili powder
Salt and freshly ground black pepper
Peanut oil
Lime slices
Toasted Pecan Butter

Rinse the catfish fillets and pat dry with paper towels.

In a shallow bowl whisk together the buttermilk, eggs, and Tabasco. In another shallow bowl combine the cornmeal, chili powder, and salt and pepper to taste. Dip each fillet into the buttermilk, then dredge in the cornmeal mixture. Shake off any excess.

Pour about 1 inch of peanut oil into a large, heavy skillet. Heat the oil until the temperature reaches approximately 360°F. (The oil is ready when a cube of white bread placed in the oil browns to a golden crisp in 45 seconds or less.) Fry the fillets until they are golden brown on both sides, about 3 or 4 minutes per side. Be sure to regulate the heat of the oil. If it is too hot, the fish will burn and not cook on the inside. If it is not hot enough, the fish will have a greasy, soggy texture. Drain fillets on absorbent paper towels.

Garnish the catfish with fresh slices of lemon. Top each fillet with Toasted Pecan Butter.

TOASTED PECAN BUTTER

⅔ cup pecans, lightly toasted and cooled (see page 7)
8 tablespoons (1 stick) butter, cut into cubes and softened
Juice of 1 lime
2 shallots, chopped
1 jalapeño pepper, seeded and chopped
3 tablespoons chopped fresh cilantro

In a food processor, combine all ingredients. Process until blended but still somewhat chunky. Place in a small serving dish and refrigerate until ready to serve.

SUCCULENT SEAFOOD JAMBALAYA

The word *jambalaya* comes from the French *jambon*, meaning ham, and the African *ya*, meaning rice. This recipe might seem a bit complex, but when you consider it's a meal in itself, it really isn't daunting. The homemade savory spice blend adds a little something extra, or *lagniappe*, as the Cajuns would say, to the recipe. This mixture can also be rubbed on chicken breasts or pork medallions before sautéing. Tasso is a well-seasoned, smoked Cajun ham; you can substitute any other smoked ham.

SERVES | 8

3 strips of bacon, chopped
4 ounces chopped tasso or other smoked ham
1 onion, chopped
1 green pepper, seeded and chopped
1 red pepper, seeded and chopped
¼ cup Worcestershire sauce
2 tablespoons apple cider vinegar
1 teaspoon Tabasco, or to taste
1 (16 ounce) can crushed tomatoes with added puree
1 (16 ounce) can tomato wedges with their juice
1 pound andouille or kielbasa sausage, thinly sliced
1 (10 ounce) package frozen sliced okra, defrosted
1 pound medium shrimp, peeled and deveined
8 ounces pasteurized crabmeat, picked over
8 ounces bay scallops, rinsed
3 cups cooked rice
3 tablespoons chopped fresh parsley
Additional Tabasco

SAVORY SPICE BLEND

2 tablespoons all-purpose flour
1 tablespoon chili powder
2 teaspoons garlic powder
1 teaspoon onion powder
1 teaspoon poultry seasoning
1 teaspoon celery seeds
½ teaspoon salt
½ teaspoon freshly ground black pepper

In a 4½-quart Dutch oven set over medium heat, cook the bacon until some of the fat is rendered. Add the tasso and continue cooking until the bacon begins to brown, about 5 minutes. Add the onion, green pepper, and red pepper. Cook for 5 minutes, stirring frequently.

Make the Savory Spice Blend: In a small bowl or custard cup combine the flour, chili powder, garlic powder, onion powder, poultry seasoning, celery seeds, salt, and pepper. Stir the spice blend into the Dutch oven and cook for 2 minutes.

Add the Worcestershire sauce, apple cider vinegar, Tabasco, crushed tomatoes, tomato wedges, and sausage. Cook for 20 minutes. Add the okra and cook for 10 minutes.

Stir in the shrimp, crabmeat, and scallops and cook for 3 minutes, or until the shrimp turn pink and begin to curl and the scallops become opaque. Stir in the cooked rice and parsley and heat through, about 2 minutes.

Serve at once, passing additional Tabasco separately.

LEMON-MARINATED LEG OF LAMB WITH MINT GREMOLATA

A leg of lamb is the perfect buffet entree when serving a number of guests, because it yields meat cooked to varying degrees of doneness, based on the thickness of the part of the leg the meat is taken from. I like to pair this lamb with Classic Caesar Salad and Indian Basmati Rice with Dried Fruit.

SERVES 6 TO 8

Juice and grated zest of 3 lemons
⅓ cup extra-virgin olive oil
⅓ cup honey
4 garlic cloves, chopped
1 tablespoon chopped fresh rosemary
½ cup chopped fresh mint
1 (5 pound) leg of lamb, boned and butterflied, with the skin, fat, and gristle removed
Extra-virgin olive oil
Mint Gremolata

In a large glass bowl or zip-top freezer bag combine the lemon juice and zest, olive oil, honey, garlic, rosemary, and mint. Add the lamb and turn to coat completely. Cover the bowl or seal the bag and place in the refrigerator. Marinate at least 3 hours or overnight, turning the lamb occasionally.

Preheat the oven to 425°F. Place the lamb on a broiler rack and roast for 10 minutes. Turn the lamb and roast for another 10 minutes, or until an instant-read meat thermometer inserted into the thickest part of the lamb reaches 125°F for rare meat. Allow the lamb to rest for 10 minutes before thinly slicing. Place on a serving platter and drizzle with extra-virgin olive oil. Scatter some of the Mint Gremolata over the lamb slices, passing the rest separately.

MINT GREMOLATA

½ cup grated lemon zest
¼ cup chopped fresh mint
2 tablespoons chopped fresh parsley
4 garlic cloves, chopped
½ cup freshly grated Parmesan cheese

In a medium bowl combine all ingredients. Store in the refrigerator for up to 3 days. The recipe makes 1 cup.

MOLASSES- AND CIDER-BASTED LOIN OF PORK

The molasses and apple cider lend a delicately sweet glaze to the pork loin. This dish is great to serve, fajita-style, to a large crowd: Put very thinly sliced pork on warm flour tortillas. Add sautéed onions and peppers and top with Southwestern Apple and Red Chile Chutney or Apple Serrano Salsa. Throw in some finely shredded cheddar and Monterey Jack cheeses. Be sure not to overcook the pork, as it will dry out and become tough.

SERVES | 8

½ cup molasses
½ cup apple cider
2 tablespoons chopped fresh rosemary
2 tablespoons chopped fresh cilantro
2 garlic cloves, chopped
4 green onions, chopped
Grated zest of 2 limes
1 (3 to 4 pound) pork loin, trimmed of visible fat
1 tablespoon peanut oil
Salt and freshly ground black pepper

In a large ceramic or glass bowl combine the molasses, apple cider, rosemary, cilantro, garlic, green onions, and lime zest. Add the pork loin and turn in the bowl to coat evenly. Cover with plastic wrap and marinate in the refrigerator for 8 hours or overnight.

Preheat the oven to 500°F. Brush a heavy roasting pan with the peanut oil and place the pork in the pan. Pour any reserved marinade over the pork. Place the roasting pan in the oven and immediately reduce the heat to 425°F. Cook the pork for 30 to 40 minutes, or until an instant-read meat thermometer inserted in the center of the meat registers 140°F. Let the meat rest for 10 minutes before slicing. Serve warm or at room temperature, with Southwestern Apple and Red Chile Chutney (page 56) or Apple Serrano Salsa (page 57).

TWO CONDIMENTS FOR PORK

SOUTHWESTERN APPLE AND RED CHILE CHUTNEY

MAKES 2 PINTS

3 Granny Smith apples, peeled and coarsely chopped

4 fresh red Anaheim chiles, seeded and chopped

1 onion, chopped

4 garlic cloves, chopped

1 cup golden raisins

1 cup dark brown sugar

1 cup apple cider vinegar

1 (12 ounce) bottle dark Mexican beer

2 tablespoons chili powder

1 tablespoon ground cumin

1 teaspoon ground cinnamon

1 teaspoon dry mustard

1 teaspoon salt

½ cup chopped fresh cilantro

½ cup lightly toasted pine nuts (see page 7)

In a 4½-quart, nonreactive saucepan mix together all the ingredients except the cilantro and pine nuts. Bring to a boil over medium-high heat, stirring often. Reduce the heat to low and simmer for 1 to 1½ hours, or until the liquid has cooked away and concentrated the flavors and the chutney is very thick. Remove from the heat and stir in the cilantro and pine nuts.

MAKE AHEAD | The chutney keeps in the refrigerator for 2 weeks, or frozen for 3 months.

APPLE SERRANO SALSA

You can substitute pineapple, mango, or diced melon for the apples in this flavorful salsa. A bonus: It's fat free.

MAKES | ABOUT 3½ CUPS

3 Granny Smith apples, halved, cored, and chopped in ½-inch dice
1 red onion, finely chopped
4 green onions, finely chopped
6 garlic cloves, chopped
4 serrano chiles or jalapeño peppers, seeded and finely chopped
¼ cup chopped fresh cilantro
¼ cup lime juice
1 teaspoon sugar
Salt and freshly ground black pepper

In a medium bowl mix together all ingredients. Let sit at room temperature for 1 hour to allow the flavors to mellow.

MAKE AHEAD | The salsa keeps in the refrigerator for 5 days. Do not freeze.

NOTE | When you make the salsa, *do all of the chopping by hand.* Using the food processor to chop will make the mixture too watery.

TRI-MUSTARD PORK

I love toting this easy, make-ahead entree to an afternoon picnic at the beach or an evening symphony in the park. It is wonderful sandwiched within Sweet Potato Buttermilk Biscuits and accompanied by Zesty Black Bean Salsa and Oven-Roasted New Potato and Artichoke Salad.

SERVES 4 TO 6

⅓ cup mustard seeds
⅓ cup apple cider vinegar
⅓ cup Dijon mustard
2 tablespoons dry mustard
4 garlic cloves, chopped
2 tablespoons chopped fresh rosemary
Salt and freshly ground black pepper
1 (2½ pound) pork tenderloin, separated into 2 halves

Preheat the oven to 400°F. Line a medium baking dish with aluminum foil and lightly coat the foil with nonstick cooking spray.

In a small bowl mix together the mustard seeds and the apple cider vinegar. Let sit for 10 minutes, or until the seeds are slightly softened. Stir in the Dijon mustard, dry mustard, garlic, rosemary, and salt and pepper to taste. Place the tenderloin halves in the prepared baking dish and spread the mustard mixture evenly over the pork.

Roast the pork for 30 to 35 minutes, or until an instant-read meat thermometer inserted in the center of the pork registers 140°F. Remove from the oven and let the meat rest for 10 minutes before thinly slicing on the diagonal. Serve slightly warm, using Zesty Black Bean Salsa (page 60) as a bed for the meat.

ZESTY BLACK BEAN SALSA

Besides being an excellent accompaniment to Tri-Mustard Pork, this salsa makes a great dip for corn tortilla chips, and is delicious wrapped in warm flour tortillas for a vegetarian burrito.

SERVES 4 TO 6

1 (15½ ounce) can black beans, rinsed and drained
½ cup medium-hot commercial salsa
1 red onion, chopped
4 green onions, finely chopped
4 garlic cloves, chopped
1 (8 ounce) can yellow corn, rinsed and drained
1 cucumber, cut in half lengthwise, seeded, and finely diced
2 or 3 jalapeño peppers, seeded and chopped
Juice of 2 limes
1 tablespoon chili powder
2 teaspoons ground cumin
1 teaspoon ground coriander
½ cup chopped fresh cilantro
Salt and freshly ground black pepper

In a large, nonreactive bowl combine all ingredients. Toss to mix very well, cover, and refrigerate until ready to serve. Serve cold or at room temperature.

HERB-CRUSTED BEEF TENDERLOIN WITH SUNSHINE BÉARNAISE SAUCE

This is the ideal dish to serve for an open-house buffet, when guests arrive at different times. Unlike a classic béarnaise sauce, this one won't separate as it sits, even in warm weather. Serve the tenderloin with Oven-Browned French Fries and Green Beans Pistou.

SERVES | 8

2 tablespoons chopped fresh parsley
2 tablespoons chopped fresh rosemary
2 tablespoons thyme leaves
4 garlic cloves, peeled and crushed with ½ teaspoon salt
1 tablespoon black pepper
3 tablespoons coarse-grained Dijon mustard
½ cup seasoned bread crumbs
¼ cup Worcestershire sauce mixed with ¼ cup beef stock or water
¼ cup dry sherry
1 (4 to 5 pound) beef tenderloin, trimmed of all visible fat
Sunshine Béarnaise Sauce

Preheat the oven to 500°F.

In a small bowl combine the parsley, rosemary, thyme, crushed garlic, pepper, mustard, bread crumbs, Worcestershire sauce mixed with stock or water, and the sherry. Stir to make a thick paste. Spread the paste over the trimmed tenderloin. Tuck the tail, or thinner end of the tenderloin, under the rest of the meat so that it will cook more evenly.

Coat a roasting pan rack with nonstick cooking spray and place in a roasting pan. Place the meat on the rack. Roast the meat for 20 minutes. Reduce the heat to 375°F and cook the meat for 15 to 20 minutes more, or until an instant read meat thermometer inserted into the thickest part of the tenderloin registers 125°F for rare. Remove from the oven and let the meat sit for 20 minutes before slicing.

Slice meat across the grain into very thin slices and place on a warmed serving platter. Serve with Sunshine Béarnaise Sauce.

SUNSHINE BÉARNAISE SAUCE

¼ cup dry white wine
¼ cup white wine vinegar
2 tablespoons brine-packed green peppercorns, drained and slightly crushed
1 teaspoon yellow mustard seeds
3 shallots, chopped
¼ cup chopped fresh tarragon, divided
2 cups sour cream
2 tablespoons prepared horseradish
2 tablespoons finely chopped dill pickle
2 tablespoons capers, rinsed and drained
1 teaspoon dry mustard
2 tablespoons chopped fresh parsley
Salt and freshly ground black pepper

In a medium saucepan over medium heat, combine the white wine, white wine vinegar, green peppercorns, mustard seeds, shallots, and 2 tablespoons of the tarragon. Bring to a boil and cook until the mixture is reduced by half, about 5 minutes. Remove from the heat and allow the mixture to cool.

Transfer mixture to a medium bowl. Add the sour cream, horseradish, dill pickle, capers, dry mustard, parsley, and the remaining 2 tablespoons of tarragon. Season to taste with salt and pepper. Cover and chill for 2 hours or overnight. Makes 2½ cups.

MAKE AHEAD | The Sunshine Béarnaise Sauce can be stored in the refrigerator for up to 1 week.

RATATOUILLE GRATIN

This gratin is an excellent vegetarian entree and also makes a wonderful side dish served with a leg of lamb or beef tenderloin. Salting the eggplant drains its bitter juices and helps the eggplant retain more texture for the finished presentation.

SERVES | 8

1 large eggplant, cut crosswise into ½-inch slices and each slice scored
Kosher salt
4 zucchini, cut into ½-inch slices
½ cup olive oil
3 onions, sliced
2 red peppers, seeded and sliced crosswise into rings
6 garlic cloves, chopped
½ cup balsamic vinegar
1 cup chopped fresh herbs, such as thyme, basil, parsley, oregano, and rosemary, divided
4 tomatoes, thinly sliced crosswise
2 cups grated Gruyère cheese
Salt and freshly ground black pepper
3 or 4 slices day-old French bread, processed to coarse crumbs
¼ cup extra-virgin olive oil

Preheat the oven to 400°F. Place the eggplant in a colander and sprinkle with the kosher salt. Leave for 30 minutes. Rinse, drain, and pat the eggplant dry.

Brush the eggplant and zucchini slices with all but 3 tablespoons of the olive oil and place them on a lightly oiled baking sheet. Bake in the oven for about 20 minutes. Set aside to cool.

Meanwhile, in a large sauté pan, heat the remaining 3 tablespoons of oil. Add the onion slices, red peppers, and garlic. Cook over medium heat until soft, about 8 to 10 minutes. Add the balsamic vinegar, ½ cup of the chopped herbs, and the baked eggplant and zucchini. Stir until heated through.

Lightly grease a 9 x 13 x 2-inch baking dish. Layer the eggplant mixture, tomatoes, Gruyère cheese, and the remaining ½ cup of herbs, adding salt and pepper to taste between each layer. Top with bread crumbs and drizzle with extra-virgin olive oil.

Bake for 1 hour, or until the top crust is golden brown and the gratin is thick and bubbly. Allow to cool 20 minutes before serving.

VERSATILE VEGETABLE SAUCE

This pasta sauce is really a basic ratatouille recipe and can be used in lots of different dishes. I have listed some of my favorites below.

MAKES | 8 CUPS

¼ cup olive oil
2 tablespoons butter
2 onions, chopped
1 red pepper, seeded and chopped
1 green pepper, seeded and chopped
4 garlic cloves, chopped
1 small eggplant, cubed (about 3 cups)
1 cup sliced fresh mushrooms
1 yellow squash, thinly sliced
1 zucchini, thinly sliced
2 carrots, peeled and shredded
1 (28 ounce) can crushed tomatoes with added puree
1 cup red wine
¼ cup balsamic vinegar
1 tablespoon fennel seed, lightly toasted
½ teaspoon red pepper flakes
¾ cup assorted chopped fresh herbs, such as parsley,
   rosemary, thyme, basil, and oregano,divided
1 tablespoon sugar
Salt and freshly ground black pepper

In a 5½-quart Dutch oven combine the olive oil and the butter. Cook over medium-high heat until hot. Add the onions, red pepper, green pepper, and garlic and cook, stirring constantly, until tender, about 5 minutes. Add the eggplant, mushrooms, yellow squash, zucchini, and carrots and cook until crisp-tender, about 5 minutes. Stir in the crushed tomatoes, red wine, balsamic vinegar, fennel seed, red pepper flakes, ½ cup of the chopped herbs, sugar, and salt and pepper to taste. Bring mixture to a boil, reduce heat to a simmer, and cook, uncovered, for 45 minutes to 1 hour, or until sauce is reduced and thick. Stir in the remaining ¼ cup of chopped herbs.

MAKE AHEAD | You can freeze this sauce for up to 6 months in 1-quart zip-top freezer bags. Defrost overnight in the refrigerator or according to your microwave instructions. Omit the final ¼ cup of fresh herbs until you reheat the sauce just before serving.

MENU IDEAS

– Toss with hot, cooked spaghetti or fettucine for a delicious pasta dish. Top with freshly grated Parmesan cheese.

– Use as a bed for grilled chicken or pork, baked fish, roast leg of lamb, or beef tenderloin.

– Use as a filling for breakfast omelets, with shredded Romano and Asiago cheese.

– Top a store-bought pizza shell with Versatile Vegetable Sauce, pepperoni slices, and mozzarella cheese. Bake at 425°F for 10 to 12 minutes.

– For an easy minestrone soup, to 1 quart of Versatile Vegetable Sauce add 8 cups of chicken stock, ⅔ cup dry macaroni, two (15½ ounce) cans rinsed and drained white beans, and a couple of tablespoons of pesto sauce. Bring to a boil, reduce the heat to low, and simmer for 10 to 12 minutes, or until the macaroni is tender.

– For savory caponata, to 1 quart of Versatile Vegetable Sauce add ½ cup each sliced green and black olives, ¾ cup seasoned bread crumbs, and ¼ cup drained capers. Heat in the oven at 350°F for 30 minutes (or in the microwave on full power for 4 to 5 minutes) until thick and bubbly. Allow to stand for 10 minutes, then drizzle with 2 tablespoons of extra-virgin olive oil and 2 tablespoons of balsamic vinegar. Serve with crackers, toasted pita wedges, or bagel chips.

– For Spanish rice casserole, to 1 quart of Versatile Vegetable Sauce add 1 (15½ ounce) can rinsed and drained pinto beans, 1 cup long-grain rice, 2½ cups beef stock, 2 tablespoons chili powder, 1 tablespoon ground cumin, and 1 teaspoon dried oregano. Cover with aluminum foil and bake at 375°F for 1 hour, or until the liquid has been absorbed and the rice is tender. Scatter the top with 4 chopped green onions just before serving.

– For vegetable burritos, to 1 quart of Versatile Vegetable Sauce add 1 (15½ ounce) can rinsed and drained black beans, 1 (8 ounce) can shoepeg corn, the juice of 1 lime, 1 tablespoon chili powder, 1 tablespoon ground cumin, ½ teaspoon red pepper flakes, and ⅓ cup chopped fresh cilantro. Heat in a sauté pan until simmering and serve spooned into warmed flour tortillas. Top with grated cheddar and Monterey Jack cheeses, shredded iceberg lettuce, chopped tomatoes, and green onions. Spoon sour cream to taste into each burrito.

PENNE BAKED WITH EXOTIC MUSHROOMS

This meatless pasta has a savory, full-flavored taste, thanks to the addition of exotic dried mushrooms. Since the pasta will continue to bake in the oven, it is best to slightly undercook it in the water so it will not become mushy.

SERVES 8

3 ounces dried exotic mushrooms

2 cups white wine

2 tablespoons butter

2 tablespoons olive oil

1 onion, chopped

1 (16 ounce) can chopped tomatoes with their juice

2 cups thinly sliced button mushrooms

2 tablespoons chopped fresh sage

2 tablespoons thyme leaves

2 cups freshly grated Parmesan cheese, divided

12 ounces penne pasta or rigatoni, cooked until barely al dente

1 cup seasoned bread crumbs

Chopped tomatoes

Chopped fresh parsley

WHITE SAUCE

⅓ cup (about 5⅓ tablespoons) butter

⅓ cup all-purpose flour

3½ cups half and half

2 egg yolks, beaten

⅛ teaspoon freshly grated nutmeg

Salt and freshly ground black pepper

In a small bowl soak the dried mushrooms with the white wine for 1 hour. Remove the mushrooms and coarsely chop. Strain the wine through a double thickness of cheesecloth and set aside.

In a large sauté pan melt the butter with the olive oil. Add the onion and cook over medium heat until the onion is soft, about 5 minutes. Stir in the chopped tomatoes with their juice, the chopped exotic mushrooms, and the filtered wine. Add the fresh mushrooms, sage, and thyme. Cook over medium-high heat until all the liquid has evaporated.

Meanwhile, make the White Sauce: In a medium saucepan melt the butter and stir in the flour. Cook over low heat, stirring constantly, for a few minutes, being careful not to brown the flour. This is called a blond roux. Stir in the half and half and bring the mixture to a boil. Add about ½ cup of the sauce to the beaten egg yolks to temper, or warm, them. Add the egg yolk mixture back into the saucepan and stir to combine. Season to taste with the nutmeg, salt, and pepper.

Stir the White Sauce into the sauté pan, along with 1 cup of the Parmesan cheese.

Preheat the oven to 400°F. In a large bowl toss together the mushroom sauce and the cooked pasta. Butter a large, oval casserole dish. Pour the sauced pasta into the prepared dish and top with the remaining 1 cup of Parmesan cheese and the bread crumbs. Bake for 20 to 25 minutes, or until a nice golden crust has developed. Let stand 10 minutes before serving. Garnish each serving with chopped tomatoes and parsley.

PHYLLO-LAYERED VEGETABLE STRUDEL

"No boil" lasagna noodles can be substituted for the phyllo dough if desired.

SERVES | 8 TO 10

3 cups part-skim ricotta cheese, drained

2 eggs, beaten

1 (10 ounce) package chopped frozen spinach, defrosted and squeezed dry

¼ cup chopped fresh parsley

½ teaspoon red pepper flakes

3 cups shredded part-skim mozzarella cheese

Salt and freshly ground black pepper

¾ cup clarified butter (see note)

12 sheets phyllo dough, defrosted

8 cups Versatile Vegetable Sauce (page 64)

1 cup freshly grated Parmesan cheese

Preheat the oven to 375°F. To make the filling, in a large bowl mix together the ricotta cheese, eggs, spinach, parsley, red pepper flakes, mozzarella cheese, and salt and pepper to taste. Set aside.

Brush a 13 x 9 x 2-inch baking dish or large lasagna pan with clarified butter. As you work with the phyllo dough, cover the portion you are not using with a moist towel to prevent it from drying out. Working with 1 sheet of phyllo at a time, brush half of the dough with clarified butter. Fold the dough in half crosswise (like a book) and brush the top of the sheet with more clarified butter. Place the folded sheet into the prepared pan. Repeat with 3 more sheets of phyllo dough, layering these on top of the other sheet, until you have 4 sheets folded to create 8 layers.

Top with half of the Versatile Vegetable Sauce and half of the ricotta mixture. Layer 4 more folded sheets on top of this, buttering each folded layer as above. Add the remaining pasta sauce and ricotta mixture. Repeat the buttering and folding of the final 4 sheets of phyllo dough, pressing the dough into the corners and the sides of the pan and trimming any excess dough with a sharp knife. Brush the top sheet of the dough with more butter and lightly score it in half lengthwise, then in fourths crosswise, to form eight squares.

Bake in the oven until the top is golden brown, about 35 minutes. Remove from the oven and sprinkle with Parmesan cheese. Bake an additional 15 minutes. Remove to a wire rack and cool 20 minutes before cutting.

To serve, cut though the scored lines and gently remove slices from the pan with a spatula.

NOTES | To clarify butter, cube ½ pound (2 sticks) of unsalted butter and place in a medium saucepan. Melt the butter over very low heat, skimming off any foam that rises to the top. When the butter has melted, remove from the heat and let sit for 3 minutes. Gently pour the butter through a double thickness of dampened cheesecloth in a wire strainer suspended over a large measuring cup, leaving the milk solids in the bottom of the saucepan. Use the butter as directed above. Leftover butter will keep for 1 month in the refrigerator.

Defrost the phyllo overnight in the refrigerator, not at room temperature. I always buy two packages of phyllo dough, one from the front of the freezer case and the second from the rear. You never know how long the phyllo has been in your grocer's freezer, and if the store doesn't rotate its inventory on a regular basis, you may get a dried-out package. Plus it's good to have some dough on hand for a little peace of mind when working with this fragile pastry. If it does happen to tear, don't fret. You can easily patch the tear by buttering and layering another piece of dough on top of the torn piece.

SIDE DISHES

White Beans with Tarragon and Niçoise Olives

Spicy Rapini Eleanora

Banana Pepper, Squash, and Corn Pudding

Zucchini Ripieni

Braised Red Cabbage with Apples

Parmesan Garlic Mashed Potatoes

Oven-Browned French Fries with Fennel and Dijon

Oven-Roasted New Potato and Artichoke Salad

Green Beans Pistou

Ray's Pesto Sauce

Minted Green Beans with Red Onion and Red Pepper

Vegetable Ribbons with Horseradish Lemon Butter

Crushed Red Potatoes with Bitter Greens

Pan-Roasted Barley Pilaf

Indian Basmati Rice with Dried Fruit

Lemon and Saffron Risotto with Asparagus Tips

Couscous with Asparagus

Thai-Style Noodles with Crunchy Vegetables

Southwestern Seasoned Rice with Black Beans

Wild Rice with Portobello Mushrooms

WHITE BEANS WITH TARRAGON AND NIÇOISE OLIVES

I like to serve this as a bed for grilled pork or veal chops, or alongside Garlic Pan-Roasted Shrimp, or ladled on top of Sour Cream and Chive Bread. Greek black olives such as kalamata can be used in place of the niçoise olives. If tarragon is unavailable, a combination of basil, oregano, and parsley makes a nice alternative.

SERVES 6 TO 8

6 slices of bacon, coarsely chopped
1 red onion, chopped
4 garlic cloves, chopped
2 ribs of celery, thinly sliced
2 carrots, peeled and shredded
⅓ cup herb-flavored vinegar, such as tarragon, basil, or thyme
2 tablespoons brown sugar
3 plum tomatoes, seeded and coarsely chopped
1 small English cucumber, cut in half lengthwise, seeded, and finely diced
Juice of 2 lemons
1 teaspoon ground coriander
3 tablespoons chopped fresh tarragon
2 (15½ ounce) cans white beans, rinsed and drained
½ cup pitted niçoise olives
Salt and freshly ground black pepper
4 green onions, finely chopped

In a large skillet cook the bacon over medium heat until crispy and golden brown, about 5 minutes. Remove and drain on paper towels.

To the hot drippings add the red onion, garlic, celery and carrots. Cook until tender, about 5 minutes. Stir in the flavored vinegar and brown sugar. Cook until the liquid has evaporated, about 3 minutes.

Transfer the contents of the skillet to a large bowl. Add the tomatoes, cucumber, lemon juice, coriander, tarragon, white beans, niçoise olives, and salt and pepper to taste. Stir in the reserved bacon. Toss to mix very well, cover, and refrigerate for 4 hours or overnight.

One hour before serving, stir the mixture very well and allow to sit at room temperature. Scatter the chopped green onions over the beans just before serving.

SPICY RAPINI ELEANORA

Rapini, sometimes called broccoli rabe (or raab) is a marvelous vegetable that resembles leafy broccoli but has a sharper, more distinctive taste. Its flavor balances well with sweet balsamic vinegar. This particular dish is named after my dear friend Nancy's mother-in-law, who first tasted (and fell in love with) this quick and easy side dish when I made it one unusually cool summer evening on Long Island.

SERVES 6 TO 8

3 pounds (about 2 large bunches) rapini
3 tablespoons olive oil
6 garlic cloves, thinly sliced
1 onion, thinly sliced
1 red pepper, seeded and thinly sliced
½ teaspoon red pepper flakes
¼ cup dry white wine
¼ cup balsamic vinegar
Salt and freshly ground black pepper

Cut off about 2 inches of the tough stalks from the bottom of the rapini and discard. Place the rapini in the basket of a steamer set over simmering water and cook for 8 to 10 minutes, or until crisp-tender. Remove from the steamer basket and set aside to cool.

In a large skillet heat the olive oil until very hot. Stir in the garlic, onion, and red pepper. Sauté for 2 or 3 minutes over medium heat, stirring constantly and being careful not to burn the garlic. Add the steamed rapini and the red pepper flakes. Toss to coat the rapini. Stir in the white wine and balsamic vinegar and cook until the liquid has evaporated, about 3 to 5 minutes. Season to taste with salt and pepper. Serve at once.

BANANA PEPPER, SQUASH, AND CORN PUDDING

Baking this delicious dish in a bain-marie, or water bath, assures a constant cooking temperature, resulting in a creamy custard that binds the different flavors together. To give this a Southwestern flair, omit the thyme leaves and add 1 tablespoon chili powder, 2 teaspoons ground cumin, ¼ teaspoon cayenne pepper, and ⅓ cup chopped fresh cilantro.

SERVES | 6 TO 8

2 tablespoons olive oil
2 banana peppers, halved, seeded, and thinly sliced
1 red pepper, seeded and chopped
4 garlic cloves, chopped
1 onion, thinly sliced
3 or 4 yellow squash, coarsely chopped (about 4 cups)
2½ cups yellow corn kernels (about 4 ears) or 1 (16 ounce) bag frozen corn kernels
3 egg yolks
3 eggs
1 cup milk
1 cup sour cream
Salt and freshly ground black pepper
Dash of freshly grated nutmeg
1 tablespoon thyme leaves
1 cup shredded sharp cheddar cheese

Preheat the oven to 375°F.

In a large skillet heat the olive oil over medium heat until sizzling. Add the banana peppers, red pepper, garlic, and onion. Cook until soft, about 5 minutes. Add the squash and corn and cook about 10 minutes, or until the squash is wilted and most of the liquid has evaporated. Set aside to cool, about 10 minutes.

In a large bowl combine the egg yolks, whole eggs, milk, sour cream, salt and pepper to taste, nutmeg, and thyme leaves. Whisk until smooth. Stir in the sautéed squash and corn mixture and the shredded cheese.

Pour into a 2½-quart buttered casserole or soufflé dish. Set the dish in a shallow roasting pan and pour 1 inch of boiling water into the pan. Bake the casserole in the water bath for 45 to 50 minutes, or until the custard is set in the center. Let cool for 10 minutes before serving.

NOTE | The easiest way to remove corn kernels from the cob is to anchor one end of a corncob on the center tube of an angel food cake pan. With a sharp knife, cut the kernels straight down. The kernels will collect in the bottom of the pan instead of flying all over the kitchen counter.

ZUCCHINI RIPIENI

These beautiful stuffed boats of zucchini resemble the Italian flag in color, while their flavor speaks of the Mediterranean. They make a wonderful first course or an elegant vegetarian main meal, paired with a simple salad and a loaf of crusty bread.

SERVES 8

3 slices white bread
4 large zucchini
3 tablespoons olive oil
2 garlic cloves, chopped
1 red onion, chopped
1 small eggplant, cut into ½-inch dice
1 cup shredded Gruyère cheese
3 tablespoons chopped fresh basil
2 ripe plum tomatoes, halved and thinly sliced
Balsamic vinegar

Preheat the oven to 400°F. In a food processor, pulse the bread until it is coarse crumbs.
Cut the zucchini in half lengthwise. Scoop out the pulp with a melon baller or grapefruit spoon, leaving about ¼-inch of pulp in the shell. Reserve the pulp.

In a large skillet heat the olive oil over medium heat. Sauté the garlic and onion until soft, about 3 minutes. Add the zucchini pulp and eggplant and cook for 6 to 8 minutes. Season to taste with salt and pepper. Stir in the bread crumbs, cheese, and basil. Stuff the zucchini boats with the filling. Top with the tomato slices. Bake in the oven until soft, about 20 minutes. Serve at once, drizzled with a splash of balsamic vinegar if desired.

BRAISED RED CABBAGE WITH APPLES

I enjoy this colorful dish year-round, sometimes with a simple roast duck or chicken, sometimes with a hearty plate of pan-fried Italian sausages. It is also a welcome bed for Tri-Mustard Pork. If desired, ¼ teaspoon of cinnamon can be added with the apples to enhance their sweetness.

SERVES 6 TO 8

8 tablespoons (1 stick) butter
1 large onion, thinly sliced
3 garlic cloves, chopped
1 head red cabbage, cored, halved, and cut into ½-inch slices
½ cup apple cider
2 Granny Smith apples, cored and cut into thin wedges
2 teaspoons caraway seed
Salt and freshly ground black pepper

In a large casserole or deep skillet melt the butter. Add the onion and garlic and cook over medium heat until soft, about 5 minutes.

Add the cabbage and apple cider, cover, and cook until the cabbage has wilted but is still crisp-tender, about 6 to 8 minutes. Remove the cover and stir in the apple wedges, caraway seed, and salt and pepper to taste. Continue to cook until the apples are soft but not mushy, about 5 or 6 minutes. Serve hot or at room temperature.

PARMESAN GARLIC MASHED POTATOES

The cream cheese and sour cream lend an undeniable lushness to these mashed potatoes. Beating the potatoes over a low heat helps to dry out excess water, so that they can more easily absorb the incredible flavors of the other ingredients and fluff to a very light consistency.

SERVES | 8

5 or 6 baking potatoes, peeled and cut into 1-inch cubes
6 garlic cloves, peeled
½ cup freshly grated Parmesan cheese
½ cup sour cream
1 (8 ounce) package cream cheese, cubed and softened
Salt and freshly ground black pepper
½ teaspoon celery seed
¼ cup freshly grated Parmesan cheese mixed with 1 teaspoon paprika

Place the potatoes and garlic in a 5½-quart saucepan with enough salted water to cover the potatoes by 1 inch. Bring to a boil and cook for 30 minutes, or until the potatoes are tender. Drain and return to the saucepan. Over medium-low heat beat the potatoes and garlic with an electric mixer. (This will help dry them out and fluff them up.) Beat in the Parmesan cheese, sour cream, and cream cheese. Season to taste with salt and pepper and sprinkle with the celery seeds. Continue beating with the mixer until smooth and creamy.

Transfer to a serving bowl and sprinkle with the Parmesan cheese and paprika mixture.

OVEN-BROWNED FRENCH FRIES WITH FENNEL AND DIJON

Simmering the potatoes in boiling water and then baking them in a hot oven produces nicely browned, very crispy potato wedges with soft, creamy interiors. These potatoes are a must to serve with Herb-Crusted Beef Tenderloin. Both dishes can be served at room temperature.

SERVES 6 TO 8

5 large baking potatoes, scrubbed
2 tablespoons butter
¼ cup olive oil
1 red onion, thinly sliced
Salt and freshly ground black pepper
2 tablespoons fennel seed, lightly crushed
2 tablespoons coarse-grained Dijon mustard
¼ cup chopped fresh parsley

Preheat the oven to 400°F. Cut each potato lengthwise into 8 wedges. Place the potatoes in a 6-quart stockpot with enough lightly salted water to cover them by 3 inches. Bring to a boil and cook for 8 to 10 minutes. Drain and set aside.

In a large casserole melt the butter with the olive oil, add the onion, and cook over medium heat for 2 minutes. Add the potato wedges and toss to coat. Generously sprinkle with salt and pepper. Place casserole in the oven and cook for 40 minutes, stirring the potatoes every 10 minutes to ensure even browning.

Remove from the oven and stir in the fennel seed and Dijon mustard. Return to the oven and cook for 15 minutes.

Just before serving, sprinkle the potatoes with parsley.

OVEN-ROASTED NEW POTATO AND ARTICHOKE SALAD

This is the most unequaled potato salad I have ever tasted and certainly epitomizes the theme of this book: the layering of flavor upon flavor to achieve a unique taste sensation. This dish goes especially well with grilled meats.

SERVES 8

8 slices bacon, chopped
12 large new potatoes, scrubbed
⅓ cup olive oil
Kosher salt
2 tablespoons balsamic vinegar
1 (12 ounce) jar marinated artichoke hearts, drained
1 pint cherry tomatoes, halved
1 red onion, thinly sliced
6 green onions, chopped
¼ cup freshly squeezed lemon juice
2 tablespoons Dijon mustard
2 tablespoons chopped fresh rosemary
Salt and freshly ground black pepper
1 cup shaved Parmesan cheese*

* *Run a vegetable peeler over a wedge of room-temperature Parmesan cheese to create long shavings.*

Preheat the oven to 400°F. In a large skillet cook the bacon over medium heat until crispy and golden brown, about 5 minutes. Remove and drain on paper towels. Quarter the potatoes and toss with the olive oil. Sprinkle with kosher salt to taste. Place the potatoes in a large casserole dish and bake until tender, about 45 minutes, stirring every few minutes to facilitate even cooking.

Place the potatoes in a large bowl and gently toss with the balsamic vinegar. Allow to cool.

Cut the artichoke hearts in halves or thirds and add to the potatoes. Stir in the cherry tomatoes, red onion, green onions, lemon juice, Dijon mustard, rosemary, and salt and pepper to taste. Toss gently.

Sprinkle the Parmesan cheese and cooked bacon over the potato mixture just before serving.

NOTE The potatoes and red onion can be quartered and skewered, then roasted on a grill earlier in the day. Toss together with the other ingredients at the last minute.

GREEN BEANS PISTOU

Pistou is the French term for pesto. It is so easy to make fresh pesto that even novice cooks now do it regularly. If time is of the essence, you can substitute a commercially prepared pesto sauce, but using the fresh version makes an extraordinary difference.

SERVES 6 TO 8

2 pounds sugar snap peas or green beans, tipped and tailed
3 tablespoons butter
1 red onion, thinly sliced
1 red pepper, seeded and cut into ¼-inch julienne
½ cup Ray's Pesto Sauce (page 85)
Salt and freshly ground black pepper
½ cup lightly toasted chopped walnuts (see page 7)
½ cup freshly grated Parmesan cheese
½ cup pitted Greek black olives

In a large stockpot bring 3 quarts of salted water to a boil. Add the sugar snap peas or green beans and cook for 5 to 6 minutes, until just crisp-tender. Drain and refresh the beans under cold, running water. Drain again and set aside.

In a large skillet heat the butter until it just begins to brown. Add the onion and red pepper and cook over medium heat until they just begin to wilt, about 3 minutes. Add the sugar snap peas or green beans and stir to coat with butter. Continue cooking until the beans are heated through, about 2 minutes. Add the pesto sauce and taste for seasoning, adding salt and pepper as desired.

Garnish with the walnuts, Parmesan cheese, and black olives before serving. This dish can be served hot or at room temperature.

NOTE You can cook the beans in the microwave. Place the beans in a heavy-duty, zip-top freezer bag. Add 1 tablespoon of water, then seal the bag but leave a 1-inch opening. Microwave at full power for 3 to 4 minutes, or until beans are crisp-tender. Drain and refresh the beans under cold running water to stop the cooking.

RAY'S PESTO SAUCE

This versatile sauce can be used as a spread on breads, tossed with pasta or steamed vegetables, stirred into soups and stews, or added to risotto.

MAKES | ABOUT 1½ CUPS

4 cups firmly packed basil leaves (about 3 bunches), washed and dried
4 to 6 garlic cloves, finely chopped
½ cup toasted pine nuts or walnuts (see page 7)
½ teaspoon salt, or to taste
½ teaspoon black pepper, or to taste
¾ cup freshly grated Parmesan cheese
½ cup extra-virgin olive oil

Place the basil leaves, garlic, pine nuts, salt, pepper, and Parmesan cheese in a food processor. Blend until smooth, scraping down the sides of the bowl as necessary.

With the machine running, slowly pour in the olive oil until it is thoroughly incorporated and mixture is smooth.

MAKE AHEAD | You can store the pesto in the refrigerator for 1 week, lightly covered with a thin layer of olive oil, or freeze for 1 month. When frozen, the pesto may darken slightly.

MINTED GREEN BEANS WITH RED ONION AND RED PEPPER

The flavors of mint and raspberry enliven this simple vegetable dish.

SERVES | 6 TO 8

2 pounds green beans, tipped and tailed
1 red onion, thinly sliced
1 red pepper, seeded and cut into ¼" julienne
2 tablespoons coarse-grained Dijon mustard
¼ cup raspberry vinegar
Salt and freshly ground black pepper
1 teaspoon sugar
¼ cup extra-virgin olive oil
¼ cup chopped fresh mint, divided

In a large stockpot bring 3 quarts of salted water to a boil. Add the green beans and cook for 5 to 6 minutes, until just crisp-tender. Drain and refresh the beans under cold running water. Drain again and set aside. (Alternatively, you can cook the beans in the microwave. See note on page 84.)

In a large bowl, toss together the green beans, red onion, and red pepper.

In a small bowl, whisk together the mustard, raspberry vinegar, salt and pepper to taste, and sugar. Slowly whisk in the olive oil until the dressing is thick and emulsified. Add half of the mint to the vinaigrette and mix well. Toss the dressing with the vegetables and sprinkle with the remaining mint just before serving.

VEGETABLE RIBBONS WITH HORSERADISH LEMON BUTTER

The vegetable ribbons can be precooked in a steamer basket for 4 to 5 minutes, but I prefer to do it in the microwave and keep the kitchen cool and the stovetop free of clutter. This colorful recipe has been adapted from one in *Gourmet* magazine.

SERVES 6 TO 8

3 tablespoons butter
3 tablespoons olive oil
2 garlic cloves, chopped
¼ cup chopped fresh parsley
Juice of 2 lemons
1 to 2 tablespoons prepared horseradish
1 large onion, thinly sliced
2 zucchini, very thinly sliced lengthwise
2 yellow squash, very thinly sliced lengthwise
3 carrots, peeled and shaved into ribbons using a vegetable peeler
½ cup chicken stock or water
Salt and freshly ground black pepper

In a large skillet melt the butter with the olive oil. When the butter and oil are sizzling, stir in the garlic and parsley. Turn off the heat and continue stirring for 1 minute. Add the lemon juice and the horseradish. Set aside.

In a microwave-safe glass bowl toss the onion, zucchini, yellow squash, and carrots with the chicken stock or water. Season to taste with salt and pepper. Cover tightly with plastic wrap. With a knife, make 3 or 4 slits in the top to allow steam to escape. Place in the microwave and cook on high power for about 3 to 4 minutes, or until the vegetables are crisp-tender. Carefully remove the wrap (away from your face) and drain the vegetables in a colander.

In the skillet with the prepared butter sauce, toss the vegetable ribbons over low heat. Transfer to a serving platter and serve at once.

NOTE To thinly slice the vegetables, you can use a mandolin or a food processor fitted with the 1 millimeter slicing disk.

CRUSHED RED POTATOES WITH BITTER GREENS

Creamy potatoes, bitter greens, sharp mustard, spicy peppers, and a hint of sweetness from sugar— the complex and unexpected layers of flavors and textures in this dish combine to make this one of my favorites. For a spicier dish, break the peppers to release the seeds.

SERVES 6 TO 8

1 pound greens, such as collard greens, mustard greens, turnip greens, or rapini
3 pounds small red potatoes, scrubbed
⅓ cup balsamic vinegar
2 tablespoons Dijon mustard
1 tablespoon yellow mustard seeds
1 tablespoon chopped fresh rosemary
3 tablespoons olive oil
3 garlic cloves, thinly sliced
3 to 6 dried hot peppers
1 to 2 tablespoons sugar
Salt and freshly ground black pepper

Remove the tough, fibrous stems and wilted leaves of the greens. Wash and rinse several times. Cut into 1-inch pieces and set aside.

Place the potatoes in a 5-quart stockpot with enough lightly salted cold water to cover the potatoes by 3 inches. Bring to a boil and cook the potatoes for 15 minutes, or until tender. Remove the potatoes with a slotted spoon, reserving the cooking water, and place in a large bowl. Crush each potato lightly with the back of a spoon or a potato masher. Toss with the balsamic vinegar, Dijon mustard, mustard seeds, and rosemary. Set aside.

Add the greens to the still simmering water and cook for 8 to 10 minutes, or until tender. Drain and set aside.

In a large skillet, wok, or sauté pan with deep sides, heat the olive oil and add the garlic and hot peppers. Cook over medium heat for about 1 minute. Stir in the drained greens and sugar and toss. Stir in the seasoned potatoes and toss until heated through, about 3 minutes. Remove the peppers if desired. Season to taste with salt and pepper. Serve at once.

PAN-ROASTED BARLEY PILAF

Toasting the barley in the butter and oil gives the finished dish a rich, nutty flavor.

SERVES | 8

2 tablespoons butter
2 tablespoons olive oil
3 cups medium pearl barley, rinsed and drained
6 shallots, thinly sliced
1 to 2 jalapeño peppers, seeded and very finely chopped
2 carrots, shredded
1½ cups thinly sliced button mushrooms
6 cups beef stock
1 cup red wine
2 tablespoons tomato paste
Salt and freshly ground black pepper
2 tablespoons chopped fresh parsley

In a 3½-quart heavy saucepan with a tight-fitting lid, heat the butter and the olive oil. Add the barley and cook, stirring often, until the barley starts to brown and gives off a rich, nutty aroma, about 10 minutes. Add the shallots, jalapeño pepper, carrots, and mushrooms. Cook until the mushrooms wilt, about 2 minutes. Add the beef stock, red wine, tomato paste, and salt and pepper to taste.

Bring to a boil, then reduce the heat to a simmer. Cover and cook for about 45 minutes, or until the liquid has been absorbed. Stir the barley just before serving and sprinkle with the chopped parsley.

VARIATION | You can substitute long-grain rice for the barley in this dish. In that case, omit the red wine and reduce the cooking time to about 20 minutes.

INDIAN BASMATI RICE WITH DRIED FRUIT

Any dried fruit can be used in this recipe with equally good results. In fact, you can now buy packets of chopped, assorted dried fruits, sometimes labeled "fruit bits," which would work well here. Toasting the curry powder with the onion and celery helps to release the natural oils in this remarkable blend of spices.

SERVES 8

8 tablespoons (1 stick) butter
1 onion, chopped
2 ribs of celery, chopped
1 tablespoon mild curry powder, preferably Madras
2½ cups basmati rice
6½ cups chicken stock
½ cup dried cranberries
½ cup golden raisins
½ cup lightly toasted sunflower seeds
2 tablespoons chopped fresh basil
Salt and freshly ground black pepper
Freshly grated nutmeg

In a 3½-quart saucepan with a tight-fitting lid, heat the butter until just beginning to brown. Stir in the onion, celery, and curry powder. Cook over medium heat, stirring occasionally, for 5 minutes. Stir in the basmati rice and cook for 3 minutes. Stir in the stock and bring to a boil. Reduce the heat to low, cover, and cook for 20 minutes.

Turn off the heat. Stir in the dried cranberries, golden raisins, sunflower seeds, basil, and salt and pepper to taste. Cover and let sit for 10 minutes. Fluff with a fork and dust with freshly grated nutmeg just before serving.

LEMON AND SAFFRON RISOTTO WITH ASPARAGUS TIPS

I especially like this dish served with Sizzling Spring Ginger Salmon, but creamy risotto lends itself equally well to chicken, beef, pork, or lamb. In fact, this dish complements just about anything and is even welcome as a vegetarian entree.

SERVES | 6 TO 8

6 cups chicken stock or vegetable stock
1 teaspoon saffron threads, crumbled
2 tablespoons olive oil
1 onion, chopped
3 garlic cloves, chopped
¼ teaspoon red pepper flakes
2 cups Arborio rice

Juice and grated zest of 3 lemons
1 cup asparagus tips or coarsely chopped
   asparagus
½ cup milk
1 cup freshly grated Parmesan cheese
Freshly ground black pepper
2 green onions, chopped

In a 2-quart saucepan bring the stock to a boil and stir in the crumbled saffron threads. Reduce the heat and keep the stock at a steady simmer.

In a large, deep-sided sauté pan, heat the olive oil. Add the onion, garlic, and red pepper flakes and cook over medium heat until soft but not brown, about 3 to 4 minutes. Add the rice to the pan and stir with a wooden spoon until the grains are well coated, about 2 minutes. Add the lemon zest and the juice and mix well.

Now begin adding the simmering stock, ½ cup at a time, to the sauté pan, stirring frequently and letting the stock become completely absorbed before adding any more liquid. Continue stirring over medium heat, adding the simmering stock ½ cup at a time, until all the stock has been used. This process should take about 20 minutes.

Add the asparagus tips and milk. Stir until the milk is nearly absorbed. Stir in the Parmesan cheese. Cover and let sit for 5 minutes.

Transfer to a serving dish and sprinkle with pepper to taste. Top with green onions and serve.

MAKE AHEAD | This dish can be made ahead and reheated in the microwave. Heat for 3 to 4 minutes at full power, stir once, and continue heating for 1 minute. It can also be frozen, tightly wrapped. Defrost overnight in the refrigerator.

COUSCOUS WITH ASPARAGUS

I always keep a box or two of couscous in the pantry, so I have it on hand whenever I need a quick dish to round out a menu.

SERVES | 8

4 cups chicken stock
1 cup dry white wine
6 green onions, chopped
1 pound pencil-thin asparagus, woody stems discarded, cut into 1-inch diagonal slices
1 red pepper, seeded and thinly sliced
Juice and grated zest of 1 lemon
2 cups couscous
Salt and freshly ground black pepper
2 tablespoons chopped fresh parsley
⅔ cup freshly grated Parmesan cheese

In a 2½-quart saucepan with a tight-fitting lid, bring the chicken stock and white wine to a boil. Add the green onions, asparagus, red pepper, lemon juice, and lemon zest. Cook for 3 to 4 minutes.

Remove from the heat, add the couscous, stir, and cover. Let sit for 5 minutes. Remove the cover and fluff the grains of couscous with a fork. Season to taste with salt and pepper. Sprinkle with the chopped parsley and Parmesan cheese just before serving.

THAI-STYLE NOODLES WITH CRUNCHY VEGETABLES

The complex flavors in this dish are reflective of typical Thai cuisine, combining sweet, salty, sour, and spicy notes. This dish is a meal in itself or a wonderful side dish to serve with fish or chicken. It is especially delicious served with Szechwan Chicken and Shrimp Brochettes.

SERVES 6 TO 8

8 ounces spaghetti or vermicelli
1 head broccoli, cut into bite-sized florets
2 carrots, cut on a diagonal in ¼-inch slices
1 tablespoon peanut or vegetable oil
1 red pepper, cut into ¼-inch julienne
2 tablespoons chopped ginger
3 garlic cloves, finely chopped
⅓ cup crunchy peanut butter

2 tablespoons soy sauce
1 tablespoon rice wine vinegar
2 teaspoons dark Asian sesame oil
1 tablespoon fish sauce
1 teaspoon brown sugar
½ teaspoon red pepper flakes
2 tablespoons sesame seeds
Juice of 1 lime

Cook the pasta according to package instructions. During the last 1 to 2 minutes of cooking time, add the broccoli and carrots. Drain and refresh under cold running water to stop the cooking process. Set aside.

In a large sauté pan or wok heat the oil over medium heat. Add the red pepper, ginger, and garlic and cook for 3 minutes, or until soft. In a small bowl whisk together the peanut butter, soy sauce, rice wine vinegar, sesame oil, fish sauce, brown sugar, and red pepper flakes. Add to the sauté pan and stir over medium heat to coat the vegetables.

Add the drained pasta, broccoli, and carrots to the sauté pan. Add the sesame seeds and toss well to coat. Heat for 1 minute. Transfer to a serving platter and squeeze the lime juice over the coated pasta and vegetables. Serve hot or at room temperature.

MAKE AHEAD | This dish will keep for several days in the refrigerator.

SOUTHWESTERN SEASONED RICE WITH BLACK BEANS

Whenever I am serving this dish with a simple cut of meat, I add 1 teaspoon of red pepper flakes to enhance the subtle flavors of the rice.

SERVES 8

⅓ cup peanut oil
2½ cups long-grain rice
1 onion, chopped
2 garlic cloves, chopped
1 (15½ ounce) can chopped tomatoes with their juice
1 tablespoon chili powder
1 teaspoon ground cumin
3½ cups beef stock
3 poblano peppers, seeded and cut into strips*
½ cup loosely packed cilantro leaves
1 (15½ ounce) can black beans, rinsed and drained
Salt and freshly ground black pepper
2 tablespoons chopped fresh cilantro

* *An 8-ounce can of mild green chiles, drained and chopped, can be substituted for the poblano peppers.*

Preheat the oven to 375°F. In a large casserole over medium heat, heat the oil until hot. Add the rice, onion, and garlic and cook until soft, about 5 minutes. Add the tomatoes, chili powder, and cumin and cook, stirring constantly, for about 5 minutes. Stir in the beef stock, poblano pepper strips, cilantro leaves, and black beans. Season to taste with salt and pepper.

Cover tightly with aluminum foil and bake for 40 minutes, or until all the liquid has been absorbed.

Just before serving, fluff the rice with a fork. Sprinkle with chopped cilantro and serve at once.

WILD RICE WITH PORTOBELLO MUSHROOMS

The crunchy, nutty texture of wild rice pairs nicely with the richness and meatiness of portobello mushrooms. This dish belongs with a simple roast chicken or rare tenderloin of beef.

SERVES | 6 TO 8

1 cup wild rice
3½ cups chicken stock
4 tablespoons butter
2 shallots, chopped
2 garlic cloves, chopped
12 portobello mushroom caps, cut into ¼-inch-thick slices
¼ cup dry sherry
2 tablespoons honey
2 tablespoons balsamic vinegar
1 tablespoon thyme leaves
Salt and freshly ground black pepper
2 tablespoons chopped fresh parsley

Place the wild rice in a strainer and rinse with cold water until the grains begin to swell and crack and the water runs clear, about 3 minutes. Place the rice in a medium saucepan with a tight-fitting lid and add the stock. Bring to a boil, reduce the heat to low, cover, and cook for 50 to 60 minutes. Fluff with a fork. Keep the rice covered to stay warm.

Meanwhile, in a large skillet, melt the butter over medium heat. Add the shallots and the garlic and cook until the shallots are translucent, about 3 minutes. Add the portobello mushrooms, dry sherry, and honey. Simmer over low heat until the liquid evaporates and the mushrooms begin to glaze and brown slightly. Stir in the balsamic vinegar and thyme leaves. Add this mixture to the cooked rice, adding salt and pepper to taste. Toss to distribute the mushrooms evenly.

Mound on a serving platter and sprinkle with parsley.

BREADS

Savory Herb and Sunflower Seed Bread

Parmesan Pepper Wreath

Lime Cumin Parmesan Wafers

Greek Black Olive and Sun-Dried Tomato Focaccia

Walnut and Black Olive Fougasse

Puff Pastry Cheese Twists

Sour Cream and Chive Bread

Wild Rice Muffins

Garlic-Thyme Corn Muffins

Rosemary and Garlic Breadsticks

Sweet Potato Buttermilk Biscuits

Caramel and Walnut Sticky Buns

SAVORY HERB AND SUNFLOWER SEED BREAD

This bread, with its crunchy texture, actually improves in flavor if allowed to sit, tightly wrapped, overnight. Be sure to allow the bread to cool completely before wrapping, or it will become soggy. Remember that fresh herbs are the key to ultimate success.

MAKES 1 LOAF

1 tablespoon yellow cornmeal (not cornmeal mix)
1 cup whole-wheat flour
2¼ to 3¼ cups bread flour
1 package RapidRise yeast
1 tablespoon sugar
3 tablespoons chopped fresh parsley
2 tablespoons chopped fresh dill
1 tablespoon chopped fresh rosemary
1 teaspoon salt
½ teaspoon black pepper
½ cup roasted, salted sunflower seeds
1 cup hot milk (125°F)
⅓ cup olive oil
2 tablespoons honey
1 egg mixed with 1 tablespoon water

Lightly coat a 9 x 5 x 3-inch loaf pan with cooking spray and sprinkle with cornmeal. Set aside.

In a large food processor fitted with the plastic dough blade, combine the whole-wheat flour, 2¼ cups of the bread flour, yeast, sugar, parsley, dill, rosemary, salt, pepper, and sunflower seeds. Pulse the machine on and off several times to combine well.

In a measuring cup or batter bowl with a 2-cup capacity, stir together the hot milk, olive oil, honey, and egg mixed with water. With the processor running, slowly pour the liquid into the work bowl, allowing the mixture to form a soft dough. This should take about 45 seconds. Add the remaining flour, in ¼-cup increments, and knead until the dough forms a

ball and is no longer sticky. With the machine running, continue to knead the dough for about 1 minute, until the dough is smooth and elastic and bounces back when gently pressed with a finger.

Place the dough in a gallon-sized zip-top freezer bag that has been sprayed with nonstick cooking spray. Set aside at room temperature and allow the dough to rise and double, about 1 hour (see note).

Remove the dough from the bag, punch down, and on a lightly floured board roll the dough into a 10 x 7-inch rectangle. Roll up the dough in a jelly-roll fashion, starting with a short side. Pinch the ends to seal and tuck them under the dough. Place the dough, seam side down, into the prepared pan. Let the dough rise in a warm place until doubled in size, about 45 minutes. Brush with the egg glaze. Preheat the oven to 375°F.

Bake the bread for 40 to 45 minutes, or until the loaf sounds hollow when tapped on the bottom. If needed, cover the bread with aluminum foil to prevent excess browning during the last 10 minutes or so. Remove from the pan and cool on a wire rack before slicing.

NOTE You can use the microwave for the bread's first rising. This method will take 21 minutes, versus 1 hour with the conventional method of rising. Place the dough in a sealed zip-top freezer bag. Put it in the microwave, along with 1 cup of hot tap water. Microwave the bread on the lowest setting (usually 10% power, but check the manufacturer's instructions) for 3 minutes. Without opening the door, let the bread rest for 3 minutes. Microwave on the lowest setting for 3 minutes. Let the bread rest for 3 minutes. Microwave on the lowest setting for 3 minutes, and let the bread rest for 6 minutes. Punch down and shape as directed.

PARMESAN PEPPER WREATH

This wreath is my base for a picnic sandwich that can serve a crowd: Slice the wreath horizontally, spread with a garlic mayonnaise, and fill with an assortment of thinly sliced meats and cheeses, roasted red peppers, and sliced olives.

MAKES 1 WREATH

1 tablespoon yellow cornmeal
  (not cornmeal mix)
1¼ cups warm water (110°F to 115°F), divided
2 packages active dry yeast
2 tablespoons sugar
1 tablespoon cracked black pepper
1 teaspoon salt

3 to 4 cups bread flour
1 egg
1 cup freshly grated Parmesan cheese
1 egg white, lightly beaten
Additional black pepper and
  cornmeal (optional)

Lightly grease a large baking sheet and dust evenly with the cornmeal. Set aside.

Place ½ cup warm water in a large mixing bowl. Sprinkle in the yeast and stir until dissolved. Add the remaining ¾ cup of water, sugar, black pepper, salt, and 1 cup of the bread flour and blend well. Let sit at room temperature for 20 to 30 minutes. Add the egg, Parmesan cheese, and enough of the remaining flour to make a soft dough.

Knead the dough on a lightly floured surface, adding any of the remaining flour, until the dough is very smooth and elastic. This will take about 8 to 10 minutes. Place the dough in a gallon-sized zip-top freezer bag that has been sprayed with nonstick cooking spray and let rise in a warm place until doubled in bulk, about 1 hour.

Remove the dough from the bag and punch down. Divide the dough into 3 equal pieces. Roll each piece into a 28-inch rope. Place the ropes side by side, pinching them together at one end. Braid the dough by alternatingly lifting the outside rope over and into the center of the other two ropes. Pinch together the opposite end. Form the braid into a circle and pinch the 2 ends together.

Preheat the oven to 375°F. Place the wreath on the prepared baking sheet and let rise until doubled in volume, about 1 hour. Brush the loaf with the egg white and sprinkle with additional black pepper and cornmeal if desired. Bake for 25 to 30 minutes, or until wreath is a nice golden brown. Remove from the oven and place on a wire rack to cool.

VARIATION | The dough can be shaped into dinner rolls (makes about 2 dozen). Place them side by side, touching, on the prepared baking sheet. Glaze as directed, but reduce the baking time to about 20 minutes.

LIME CUMIN PARMESAN WAFERS

This perfect party cracker is wonderful with all kinds of dips and spreads, especially Pecan-Smoked Trout Spread.

MAKES | ABOUT 4 DOZEN CRACKERS

2 cups freshly grated Parmesan cheese
1½ cups all-purpose flour
Grated zest of 2 limes
1 tablespoon ground cumin
1 teaspoon chili powder
½ teaspoon cayenne pepper
½ teaspoon salt
10 tablespoons (1¼ sticks) cold butter, cut into ¼-inch cubes
⅓ cup freshly squeezed lime juice

In a food processor combine all ingredients. Process until the mixture is well combined and holds together when squeezed with your hand.

Remove the dough to a lightly floured surface and knead gently to form a stiff dough. Shape the dough into a log about 10 inches long and 1½ inches in diameter. Wrap in plastic wrap and refrigerate until firm, at least 2 hours or up to 24 hours.

Preheat the oven to 375°F.

Remove the dough from the refrigerator and slice into ¼-inch-thick slices. Arrange the slices about 1 inch apart on very lightly greased baking sheets. Bake them in batches for about 15 to 18 minutes, or until the edges appear crispy and brown.

Remove the crackers from the oven and allow them to cool on the baking sheets for about a minute, then transfer them to wire racks to cool completely. Store in an airtight container for 1 week or freeze.

MAKE AHEAD | I like to make several batches of dough at once and store the shaped logs, tightly wrapped, in my freezer, where they keep for up to 2 months. At a moment's notice, I can slice and bake a fresh batch of these flavorful wafers.

GREEK BLACK OLIVE AND SUN-DRIED TOMATO FOCACCIA

The black olives and sun-dried tomatoes impart a Mediterranean flavor to this "hearth bread." It is perfect served with pasta, paired with a soup or salad for a light lunch, or served with drinks before dinner.

MAKES 2 FOCACCIAS

DOUGH

1 package active dry yeast
1 cup warm water (115°F)
1 tablespoon sugar
¼ cup olive oil
2½ to 3½ cups bread flour
1 teaspoon salt

TOPPING

¼ cup olive oil
2 red onions, thinly sliced
1 fennel bulb, thinly sliced
6 garlic cloves, chopped
¼ cup balsamic vinegar
3 tablespoons chopped fresh rosemary
Kosher salt and freshly ground black pepper
1 cup freshly grated Parmesan cheese
¾ cup Greek black olives, pitted and halved, rinsed and drained
¾ cup thinly sliced, oil-packed sun-dried tomatoes

Preheat the oven to 400°F. In a measuring cup with a 2 cup capacity, combine the yeast, water, and sugar. Stir to dissolve the yeast. Let the mixture proof for 10 minutes (see note). Add ¼ cup of olive oil and stir.

In a large food processor fitted with the dough blade, combine 2½ cups of the flour and the salt. With the processor running, pour the yeast mixture in slowly until it is absorbed by the flour. Knead until the dough forms a ball and is smooth and elastic, adding more flour in ¼-cup increments as needed.

Lightly grease two baking sheets. Divide the dough in half and roll each half into an oval measuring about 10 inches long and ¾ inches thick. Place the ovals on the baking sheets and press small indentations all over the dough with your fingers. Set aside.

In a large skillet heat ¼ cup of olive oil and add the red onions, fennel, and garlic. Cook over medium heat until soft and just beginning to brown, about 15 minutes. Remove from the heat and add the vinegar, rosemary, and salt and pepper to taste.

Divide the mixture evenly between the two ovals and bake the loaves for about 15 minutes. Remove from the oven and top with Parmesan cheese, Greek olives, and sun-dried tomatoes. Return to the oven and cook for about 10 minutes more, or until golden brown and crispy around the edges. Move to a rack to cool briefly. Cut into squares or wedges. Serve warm or at room temperature.

MAKE AHEAD | These loaves freeze very well. Defrost overnight at room temperature, tightly wrapped, and reheat at 350°F for 10 to 15 minutes.

NOTE | Proofing is actually proving that the yeast is still active and alive. It should become foamy and bubbly when combined with the warm water and sugar. If it doesn't, it means that the yeast is no longer active. You will need to start again with a fresh package of yeast.

WALNUT AND BLACK OLIVE FOUGASSE

This bread resembles a leaf when baked and makes a stunning presentation served on a wooden cutting board, ready to be broken apart at the table and enjoyed. I like to serve this with additional walnut oil (or olive oil) poured onto a small bread plate and topped with freshly grated Parmesan cheese and cracked black pepper.

MAKES 1 LOAF

2½ to 3½ cups bread flour
½ cup whole-wheat flour
½ cup wheat germ
1 cup lightly toasted walnuts (see page 7), chopped
1 package RapidRise yeast
1 teaspoon salt
1 tablespoon sugar
1¼ cups hot water (120°F)
⅓ cup walnut oil
1 cup pitted, chopped Greek black olives
1 tablespoon cornmeal (not cornmeal mix)
1 egg mixed with 1 tablespoon water

In a heavy-duty stand mixer with the paddle attachment, combine 2½ cups of the bread flour, the whole-wheat flour, wheat germ, walnuts, yeast, salt, and sugar. Add the hot water, then the walnut oil and black olives. Mix for 1 minute, or until very well combined. Remove the paddle and attach the dough hook. Knead to make a soft dough, adding more flour as necessary in ¼-cup increments, for 8 to 10 minutes.

The dough is ready when it is smooth and elastic and bounces back when pressed with a finger. Place the dough in a gallon-sized zip-top freezer bag that has been lightly coated with nonstick cooking spray, seal the bag, and let the dough double in volume, about 40 minutes. Punch down (you can leave the dough in the bag) and let rise a second time, about 30 minutes. (This second rise helps to develop flavor as well as texture.)

Sprinkle a large baking sheet with the cornmeal. On a lightly floured board, punch down the dough again and roll into a 14 x 8-inch oblong shape. Transfer the dough to the prepared baking sheet.

With a sharp knife, make incisions in the dough to resemble the veins of a leaf. Pull the dough apart at these incisions. Let rise once more for about 30 minutes. Lightly brush the dough with the egg glaze.

Preheat the oven to 425°F. Place baking sheet on the middle rack of the oven. Place a small cake pan of boiling water on the bottom rack. This will produce steam and yield a crusty bread with a soft interior. Bake 25 to 30 minutes, until loaf is crisp and the bottom sounds hollow when tapped. Cool on a wire rack.

NOTE The dough can be divided into 2 loaves and rolled into two 10 x 6-inch loaves. Decrease baking time to 20 to 25 minutes.

PUFF PASTRY CHEESE TWISTS

These little make-ahead finger foods remind me of classic Southern cheese straws, but without all the fuss and with so much more flavor from the dried spices sprinkled over the pastry.

MAKES | ABOUT 3 DOZEN

1 package (2 sheets) frozen puff pastry, thawed
1 egg white mixed with 2 tablespoons water, lightly beaten
1½ cups finely grated cheese (cheddar, Swiss, Parmesan, or any combination)
½ teaspoon cayenne pepper
½ teaspoon garlic powder
½ teaspoon onion powder
½ teaspoon celery seed
½ teaspoon ground coriander
½ teaspoon ground cumin

Preheat the oven to 425°F. Lightly coat a baking sheet with nonstick cooking spray. Set aside.

On a lightly floured surface, unfold the pastry sheets and brush them all over with the egg-white mixture. Sprinkle half the grated cheese over each sheet. Fold the sheets in half crosswise and flatten with a rolling pin. Brush the tops with the remaining egg white and sprinkle with the remaining cheese.

In a small bowl mix together the cayenne pepper, garlic powder, onion powder, celery seed, coriander, and cumin. Sprinkle the dry ingredients over the cheese. Fold and flatten once more, then press the edges together to seal.

Cut each sheet crosswise into thin strips, about ¾ inches wide, and twist each strip in opposite directions several times. Place on a lightly greased baking sheet and bake for about 15 to 18 minutes. With a spatula, remove the twists to a wire rack to cool.

MAKE AHEAD | These freeze beautifully, tightly wrapped, for about 2 months.

SOUR CREAM AND CHIVE BREAD

The natural affinity between sour cream and chives makes this one of my all-time favorite bread recipes. The sour cream yields a very moist interior, and the chives offer the barest hint of sweet onions. You can substitute the green part of fresh scallions if fresh chives are unavailable. This complements any entree or pasta dish.

MAKES 1 LOAF

4 cups bread flour
2 teaspoons sugar
1 teaspoon salt
1 teaspoon black pepper
1 package RapidRise yeast
2 tablespoons olive oil
1 egg, lightly beaten
1 cup sour cream
¾ cup hot water (120°F)
¼ cup freshly snipped chives
1 egg mixed with 1 tablespoon water

In a large bowl combine 3 cups of the flour, the sugar, salt, pepper, and yeast. Make a well and in the center add the olive oil, egg, sour cream, and hot water. Stir to combine. On a large cutting board or kitchen counter pour the remaining cup of flour in a large circle. Place the wet dough in the center of the flour and with the heel of your floured hand, knead the dough until it becomes very smooth and elastic, about 12 to 15 minutes, incorporating additional flour as needed. Knead in the snipped chives until evenly distributed throughout the dough. The bread dough should be very smooth and elastic and bounce back when lightly pressed with a finger. Place the dough in a gallon-sized zip-top freezer bag that has been sprayed with nonstick cooking spray or in an oiled bowl, turning to coat the dough with the oil. Seal or cover and let rise until the dough has doubled in bulk, in 1 hour (see note).

Punch down the dough and shape into a round, placing it on a lightly greased baking sheet. Do not cover the dough. Let double again in a warm, draft-free place, about 45 minutes.

Preheat the oven to 350°F. Brush the loaf with the egg glaze, slash the top with a sharp knife in a decorative pattern if desired, and bake in the middle of the oven for about 30 minutes, or until the bottom sounds hollow when tapped. (An instant-read thermometer inserted into the center of the bread should register 190°F after about 20 seconds.) Cool on a wire rack.

MAKE AHEAD | The bread freezes well, wrapped tightly with heavy-duty foil, for up to 3 months.

NOTE | You can use the microwave for the bread's first rising. See page 101.

WILD RICE MUFFINS

These savory muffins have a wonderful crunch that comes from the cornmeal and the wild rice. They are a pleasing complement to chicken, pork, or lamb, or served with bacon, fried potatoes, and eggs for a special weekend breakfast. Any dried fruit can be substituted for the cherries; dried cranberries are especially nice.

MAKES 24 MUFFINS

⅔ cup wild rice, rinsed in a colander for 3 minutes
2⅔ cups chicken stock
2½ cups all-purpose flour
½ cup yellow cornmeal (not cornmeal mix)
¼ cup sugar
1 tablespoon baking powder
Salt and freshly ground black pepper
4 eggs, lightly beaten
½ cup milk
1 (8 ounce) container sour cream
4 tablespoons butter, melted
1 cup dried cherries

In a medium saucepan combine the rinsed wild rice and chicken stock. Place over medium-high heat and bring to a boil. Reduce the heat to low, cover the pan, and cook for 45 minutes, or until the rice is tender and the stock has been absorbed. Set aside to cool.

Preheat the oven to 400°F. Lightly coat two 12-count muffin tins with nonstick cooking spray.

In a large bowl combine the flour, cornmeal, sugar, baking powder, and salt and pepper to taste.

In a separate bowl whisk together the eggs, milk, sour cream, and melted butter. Pour the wet mixture over the dry ingredients and stir in the cooked wild rice and dried cherries. With a spoon, stir the mixture just until all the ingredients are moistened. Do not overmix.

Divide the batter among the prepared tins, filling each about ⅔ full. Bake for 20 to 25 minutes, or until the muffins are browned. Remove to a wire rack to cool slightly. Carefully loosen the edges of the muffins with a sharp knife before unmolding. Serve warm, with butter and honey.

GARLIC-THYME CORN MUFFINS

These flavorful muffins are at their best served with a hearty bowl of soup or as a substitute for fried hush puppies served with fish. Be sure not to overmix the batter, as this will toughen the muffins.

MAKES | 36 MINI-MUFFINS

2 cups yellow cornmeal (not cornmeal mix)
½ cup all-purpose flour
1 tablespoon sugar
1 tablespoon baking powder
½ teaspoon baking soda
1½ cups buttermilk
2 eggs, lightly beaten
2 tablespoons melted butter, vegetable oil, or bacon drippings
6 slices bacon, fried, drained on paper towels, and crumbled (optional)
1 cup fresh corn kernels with their milk, about 2 ears (see page 77)
6 garlic cloves, chopped
2 tablespoons thyme leaves
2 teaspoons poultry seasoning

Preheat the oven to 400°F. Grease and flour three 12-count mini-muffin tins and set aside.

In a large bowl sift together the cornmeal, flour, sugar, baking powder, and baking soda. Stir in the buttermilk and the eggs, being careful not to overmix. Add the melted butter, bacon, corn kernels, garlic, thyme leaves, and poultry seasoning. Stir just to blend the ingredients together.

Fill the prepared tins about ⅔ full and bake for 15 to 20 minutes, or until a toothpick inserted into the center of the muffins comes out clean. Place the tins on a wire rack to begin cooling. After 5 minutes, remove from the tins and continue cooling on a wire rack.

MAKE AHEAD | These muffins freeze very well for 2 to 3 months if tightly wrapped.

ROSEMARY AND GARLIC BREADSTICKS

Serve these crispy breadsticks in an oblong bread basket or standing in an attractive vessel such as a tall vase or cut-glass biscuit barrel. I usually serve these before dinner, with thin slices of prosciutto wrapped around each breadstick and an assortment of zesty Italian salad peppers or marinated vegetables.

MAKES 5 TO 6 DOZEN BREADSTICKS

2 packages active dry yeast
1¼ cups warm water (115°F)
2 tablespoons sugar
½ cup olive oil
3 to 4 cups bread flour
1 cup whole-wheat flour
½ cup wheat germ
2 teaspoons salt
1 teaspoon cracked black pepper
6 garlic cloves, chopped
4 green onions, chopped
2 tablespoons chopped fresh rosemary
Yellow cornmeal (not cornmeal mix), for dusting baking sheets
1 egg mixed with 1 tablespoon water

In a measuring cup with a 2-cup capacity combine the yeast, water, and sugar. Stir to dissolve the yeast. Let the mixture proof for 10 minutes. Add the olive oil and stir to combine. Set aside.

In a large food processor fitted with the plastic dough blade combine 3 cups of the bread flour, the whole-wheat flour, wheat germ, salt, black pepper, garlic, green onions, and rosemary. With the processor running, pour in the yeast mixture and knead until smooth and elastic, adding the remaining bread flour in ¼-cup increments as needed, until the dough forms a ball and is no longer sticky. After the dough reaches this point, continue to knead in the processor for an additional minute. Place the dough in a gallon-sized zip-top freezer bag that has been coated with nonstick cooking spray and let double in volume, about 1 hour (see note on page 101).

When the dough has doubled, remove it from the bag and divide the dough in half. Working with ½ of the dough at a time, on a lightly floured surface roll out the dough as thinly as possible. Cut the dough into strips about the width of a pencil and about 12 to 14 inches long. Twist the ends of the dough in opposite directions and place about 1 inch apart on baking sheets that have been sprinkled with cornmeal. Let double once more. This will take about 30 minutes.

Preheat the oven to 400°F.

After the dough has risen, brush the breadsticks with the egg wash. Bake for 20 to 25 minutes, or until the breadsticks are browned and crispy. Remove to a wire rack to cool completely.

SWEET POTATO BUTTERMILK BISCUITS

These extraordinary biscuits develop a crisp exterior, yet remain moist on the inside. They are divine with melted butter and honey, or opened like a sandwich and filled with thinly sliced Molasses- and Cider-Basted Loin of Pork or Tri-Mustard Pork.

MAKES 1 DOZEN BISCUITS

1 cup pureed sweet potato* or canned solid pack pumpkin (not pie filling)
½ cup buttermilk
3 cups self-rising flour, divided
½ teaspoon salt

1 tablespoon brown sugar
½ teaspoon black pepper
4 tablespoons very cold butter, cut into small cubes
2 tablespoons very cold shortening

Wash 1 large sweet potato very well, prick several times with a fork, and place in the microwave on full power for 8 to 10 minutes. (Alternatively, you can bake the sweet potato at 400°F for 1 hour.) Cool, peel, and mash the potato with a fork or in a food processor.

Preheat the oven to 450°F. Whisk the pureed sweet potato with the buttermilk and set aside.

In a large bowl combine 2 cups of the self-rising flour, salt, brown sugar, and pepper. With a pastry blender (or use 2 forks, 2 knives, or a whisk), cut in the butter and shortening until the mixture resembles a coarse meal. Shake the bowl occasionally so that the larger pieces will come to the top of the mixture, then work those to a consistent size. The pieces of fat should be about the size of green peas.

Add the sweet potato-buttermilk mixture and stir only until the dough is well combined and holds together. (It will be wet and sticky.) Do not overwork the dough. Sprinkle about ¼ cup of the reserved flour over the top of the dough, turn the dough over, and sprinkle another ¼ cup of flour over it.

With the remaining flour, flour your hands well and pinch off a piece of dough about the size of an egg. Dip the wet part of the dough into any remaining flour and gently knead by rolling the dough in your hand to form a ball. The outside of the dough should not be sticky, but the inside should be very wet. Flatten the biscuit slightly and place on a lightly greased baking sheet. Repeat with the remaining dough, placing the biscuits so that they barely touch on the baking sheet.

Bake until golden brown, about 16 to 18 minutes. Remove the biscuits to a wire rack and cool slightly. Serve at once.

MAKE AHEAD These biscuits keep in the freezer, tightly wrapped, for 3 months.

CARAMEL AND WALNUT STICKY BUNS

When I bake these, my whole house is infused with the aroma of sugar and spice. Nothing can compare to these nutty, sweet, sticky buns, whether they are served for brunch, dessert, or an afternoon snack. This is one of those comfort foods I couldn't live without.

MAKES | 18 BUNS

TOPPING

8 tablespoons (1 stick) butter
1 cup brown sugar
1 teaspoon ground cinnamon
1 cup chopped walnuts

DOUGH

3 to 4½ cups bread flour
2 tablespoons sugar
1 package RapidRise yeast
¾ teaspoon salt
¾ cup hot milk (125°F)
4 tablespoons butter, melted
1 egg

FILLING

4 tablespoons butter, softened
½ cup sugar
1 tablespoon ground cinnamon
1 cup finely chopped walnuts

Over medium-low heat, melt together the 8 tablespoons of butter, brown sugar, and 1 teaspoon of cinnamon in a 13 x 9 x 2-inch heavy baking pan. Stir in 1 cup of walnuts and set the pan off the heat.

In a food processor combine 3 cups of the bread flour, 2 tablespoons of sugar, yeast, and salt. Pulse the machine on and off to mix the ingredients very well.

In a measuring cup with a 2-cup capacity combine the heated milk and the 4 tablespoons of melted butter. With the food processor running, slowly pour this milk mixture into the dry ingredients. Add the egg and process until well combined. Add the remaining flour, in ¼-cup increments, until the dough is no longer sticky and cleans the sides of the workbowl when the machine is running. Knead the dough for 45 seconds to 1 minute more, or until it is very smooth and elastic and bounces back at you when pressed with your finger.

Remove the dough to a lightly floured surface. Cover and let rest for about 15 minutes. Roll the dough into a 12 x 18-inch rectangle. Brush the dough with the 4 tablespoons of softened butter, coming to within ½ inch of the edges of the dough.

In a small bowl, combine ½ cup of sugar, 1 tablespoon of cinnamon, and 1 cup of walnuts. Sprinkle this mixture evenly over the butter-brushed dough, lightly pressing the walnuts into the dough. Beginning at a long side of the rectangle, roll the dough up very tightly, as you would a jelly roll. Pinch the seams to seal.

With a serrated knife slice the dough into 18 pieces and place, cut sides up, in the baking pan that contains the topping. Let rise for 30 minutes, or until doubled in volume.

Preheat the oven to 375°F. Bake the buns for 25 to 30 minutes, or until the tops are a light golden brown. Remove from the oven and allow to sit for 2 minutes. Carefully invert the buns onto a large serving platter, scraping any of the topping from the bottom of the pan onto the rolls. Serve warm or at room temperature.

DESSERTS

Double Dutch Chocolate Meringue Pie

Champagne-Poached Pears

Basic Flaky Pie Crust

Pear, Black Pepper, and Walnut Tart

Rhubarb and Peach Cobbler

Very Berry Nonfat Frozen Yogurt

Parisian Galette with Spiced Fruit

Gingered Plum Crisp

Orange Almond Madeleines

Golden Nut Biscotti

Caramel and Spice Citrus Fruit

Frosted Kahlua Brownies

Rosemary Cardamom Shortbread Cookies

The Absolute Best, All-Time Favorite Chocolate Chip Cookies

German Chocolate Tartlets

Perfect Butter Pound Cake

Pumpkin Spice Roulade

Totally Decadent Fudge Cake

Fresh and Dried Apple Spice Cake with Gingered Sour Cream Topping

Pineapple Upside-Down Gingerbread

Extraordinary Ricotta Cheesecake

Strawberries Balsamico

DOUBLE DUTCH CHOCOLATE MERINGUE PIE

This is the smoothest, creamiest pie I have ever tasted. One slice of this double rich chocolate pie, and the troubles of the day simply melt away. Some people rely on chicken soup for whatever ails them. Give me this pie any day!

SERVES 8

1 Basic Flaky Pie Crust, prebaked
   (page 124)
1¼ cups sugar
¼ cup cornstarch
¼ cup Dutch-process cocoa powder
¼ teaspoon ground cinnamon
Dash of salt

2 cups milk
4 egg yolks
2 (1 ounce) squares semisweet chocolate,
   chopped
1 tablespoon butter
2 teaspoons vanilla extract

MERINGUE

4 egg whites
¼ teaspoon cream of tartar
⅓ cup sugar

Preheat the oven to 350°F.

In a 2½-quart saucepan combine the sugar, cornstarch, cocoa powder, cinnamon, and salt. Mix well. Whisk the milk with the egg yolks and gradually stir into the sugar mixture, mixing well.

Cook over medium heat, stirring constantly, until thickened and bubbly, about 8 minutes. Remove from the heat and stir in the chocolate, butter, and vanilla. Stir until the chocolate and butter have melted and are fully incorporated. Pour into the prebaked pie shell.

In a clean bowl beat the egg whites and the cream of tartar with an electric mixer at high speed for 1 minute. Gradually add the sugar, a little bit at a time, beating until soft peaks form and can hold their shape and the sugar has dissolved. Spread the meringue over the filling, sealing to the edge of the pastry. Bake for 10 to 12 minutes, or until the meringue is golden brown. Let cool before serving.

CHAMPAGNE-POACHED PEARS

This elegant dessert is quick and easy, and makes a wonderful finale when paired with Rosemary Cardamom Shortbread Cookies. A dry red or white wine can be used in place of the champagne. Red wine infuses the finished dessert with a beautiful blush of color.

SERVES | 4 TO 6

4 to 6 Bosc pears, peeled with the stem on, cut flat on the bottom
3 to 6 cups dry champagne or white grape juice
1 cinnamon stick
1 vanilla bean, split lengthwise
1 cup sugar

Place the pears in a straight-sided, narrow, heavy saucepan. The pears should not touch one another or the sides of the pan. Pour in enough champagne or white grape juice to cover the pears. Place a round cake rack on top of the pears to keep them immersed. Add the cinnamon stick and vanilla bean.

Bring to a boil. Reduce the heat to a simmer, cover, and cook for 5 minutes. Turn off the heat and allow the pears to cool in the liquid. When cool, carefully remove the pears and refrigerate.

Meanwhile, add the sugar to the cooled liquid, bring to a rolling boil, and cook until the champagne is reduced and very thick and glossy, about 20 minutes. (You may want to transfer the liquid to a large skillet to speed up the reduction.) Remove the vanilla bean and cinnamon stick and discard.

Drizzle the chilled pears with the warm glaze.

MAKE AHEAD | The pears may be made several days in advance and stored in the refrigerator in the reduced poaching liquid.

BASIC FLAKY PIE CRUST

A truly flaky pie crust is often considered the sign of an accomplished baker, yet it is easier to achieve than most people realize. All it takes is a little practice and the following guidelines: (1) use a "low protein" or gluten flour; (2) keep the shortening and butter as cold as possible; and (3) do not overwork or handle the dough too much, so it does not become tough.

MAKES | ONE 9-INCH PIE SHELL

1¼ cups all-purpose soft winter wheat flour (such as White Lily)
½ teaspoon salt
¼ cup shortening, chilled
4 tablespoons butter, chilled and cut into small cubes
3 to 6 tablespoons iced water

Mix the flour and salt together in a bowl. Cut in the shortening with a pastry blender or fork until the mixture resembles coarse cornmeal. Cut in the butter until it is about the size of small peas. Add the iced water, a little at a time, tossing the mixture with the pastry blender or fork until it is moist and holds together. (Alternately, use a food processor to make the dough: Put the flour-salt mixture in the work bowl. Add the shortening and briefly pulse, about 8 to 10 times. Add the butter and briefly pulse, about 6 to 8 times. Add the iced water, a little at the time, and pulse just until the mixture begins to form a ball.) Gather dough into a ball and flatten into a round disc. Wrap the dough in plastic wrap and let it rest in the refrigerator for 30 minutes to 1 hour.

To roll, flour a work surface and a rolling pin. Start in the center of the dough, lightly press down, and, using even pressure, roll away from you to the edge of the dough. Bring the rolling pin back to the center of the dough and proceed as above, rolling toward you this time. Turn the dough one-quarter turn and re-flour the work surface as needed. Repeat the rolling procedure above, turning the dough one-quarter turn after each complete roll until you have a round measuring approximately 13 inches in diameter.

Fold the dough round in half, then in half again, and carefully position it in the center of a 9-inch pie pan. Gently unfold and press into the pan, being careful not to stretch the dough. Alternatively, roll the dough around the rolling pin and gently unroll over the pie pan. The dough should easily drape into the pan. Trim the top crust, leaving a 1-inch overhang, and fold the overhang under the crust. Crimp the edge decoratively with the tines of a fork or form a scallop pattern using your fingers. Place the pie shell in the freezer for 30 minutes to chill before baking.

To prebake a pie shell: Preheat the oven to 400°F. Crumple a piece of waxed paper, then spread it over the crust. Fill the crumpled paper with dried peas, beans, or rice. Bake for 15 minutes. Carefully remove the waxed paper and rice, beans, or peas. (These can be saved and used again and again.) If your recipe calls for baking the filling, add it at this point. If the filling requires no cooking in the oven prick the bottom of the crust with the tines of a fork. Bake the pie shell 10 minutes longer, then cool and fill as desired.

PEAR, BLACK PEPPER, AND WALNUT TART

This delicious tart gets a surprising kick of flavor from freshly cracked black pepper. The pepper balances nicely with the warmth and sweetness of the cinnamon. A tart apple such as Granny Smith can be substituted for the pears.

SERVES | 8

1 recipe dough from Basic Flaky Pie Crust (page 124)
½ cup finely ground walnuts
2 tablespoons all-purpose flour
½ cup brown sugar
½ teaspoon freshly cracked black pepper
½ teaspoon ground cinnamon
2 ripe Bosc pears, peeled, cored, and grated
1 egg, lightly beaten
5 tablespoons butter, melted, divided
1 Bosc pear, peeled, cored, and thinly sliced
¼ cup sugar

Preheat the oven to 400°F.

Roll out the dough into an 8- or 9-inch tart tin with a removeable bottom.

In a medium bowl toss together the walnuts, flour, brown sugar, black pepper, cinnamon, grated pears, egg, and 4 table-spoons of melted butter. Spread the mixture evenly into the tart tin. Arrange the sliced pear on top of the mixture in concentric circles, overlapping in the center of the tart. Brush the pear with the remaining tablespoon of melted butter and sprinkle with the sugar.

Bake the tart for 45 to 50 minutes, or until golden. Remove to a wire rack to cool.

Unmold the tart onto a serving platter and serve warm, sliced into wedges.

NOTE | If desired, make a simple glaze by melting ⅓ cup apple or apricot jelly with 1 tablespoon freshly squeezed lemon juice until smooth. Glaze the warm tart as it cools on the wire rack.

RHUBARB AND PEACH COBBLER

We usually think of pies when we think of rhubarb, but I prefer it in this simple, rustic cobbler. The leaves and roots of the rhubarb are poisonous and should be discarded. If fresh peaches are not available, you can substitute frozen slices. Strawberries also team very nicely with the tartness of the rhubarb and can be substituted for the peaches.

SERVES 8 TO 10

FRUIT FILLING

2 pounds rhubarb, leaves and roots discarded (about 4 cups sliced)
2 pounds peaches, peeled, pitted, and sliced (about 3 cups)
1 cup chopped walnuts
1 cup sugar
⅓ cup cornstarch
Grated zest of 2 oranges

COBBLER TOPPING

2½ cups all-purpose flour
½ teaspoon salt
2 tablespoons baking powder
2 teaspoons ground coriander
Freshly grated nutmeg

¼ cup sugar
8 tablespoons (1 stick) butter,
    cut into small cubes and chilled
1½ cups heavy cream
2 teaspoons vanilla extract

Preheat the oven to 375°F. Lightly butter a 13 x 9 x 2-inch baking dish. Set aside.

Wash the rhubarb well, cutting off any brown spots. Cut the rhubarb into ½-inch slices. In a large bowl combine the rhubarb, peaches, walnuts, sugar, cornstarch, and orange zest. Toss to coat completely. Pour the fruit into the prepared baking pan.

Make the topping: In a large bowl mix together the flour, salt, baking powder, coriander, nutmeg, and sugar. With a pastry blender (or use 2 knives or 2 forks) cut in the butter until it resembles coarse meal. Add the cream and the vanilla and stir until the dry ingredients are just moistened.

Cover the fruit with dollops of the cobbler topping. Bake for 40 to 45 minutes, or until the topping is golden and the fruit is bubbling. Let cool on a wire rack for 20 minutes before serving.

VERY BERRY NONFAT FROZEN YOGURT

This frozen yogurt is better than any you will ever buy at the grocery store. I always keep a container of yogurt cheese in my refrigerator so this refreshing dessert can be ready in an instant. This is completely fat-free.

MAKES 1 QUART

1 pound frozen berries, such as strawberries, blueberries, or raspberries
   (or a mixture of all three)
½ cup confectioners' sugar
Juice and grated zest of 1 lemon
½ teaspoon vanilla extract
1 (24 ounce) container plain nonfat yogurt*, drained overnight in the refrigerator in a sieve or
   yogurt strainer lined with cheesecloth and suspended over a bowl to yield 12 to 16
   ounces of yogurt cheese
Fresh berries and mint sprigs (optional)

* *Choose a plain nonfat yogurt that does not have added gelatin in the list of ingredients. The gelatin acts as a thickener and prevents the curds of the yogurt from separating from the whey.*

In a food processor combine the frozen berries, confectioners' sugar, lemon juice, lemon zest, and vanilla. Process until finely chopped. Immediately add the drained yogurt (yogurt cheese) to the berries and process for about 30 seconds, or until the mixture freezes.

For soft-serve frozen yogurt, serve at once, or place in a freezer-proof container and let ripen tightly covered in the freezer for 3 to 4 hours. Let the frozen yogurt sit at room temperature for about 5 minutes before serving.

Serve with fresh berries sprinkled on top and garnished with mint sprigs.

PARISIAN GALETTE WITH SPICED FRUIT

This classic French dessert is also wonderful as a pastry for brunch or served with afternoon tea. If you like, add 1 tablespoon of chopped, crystallized ginger to the fruit mixture as it is cooling.

SERVES 8

1¾ to 2½ cups bread flour
1 package RapidRise yeast
½ teaspoon salt
¼ cup sugar
Grated zest of 2 oranges
½ cup sour cream
1 egg, lightly beaten
½ cup hot milk (120°F)
8 tablespoons (1 stick) butter
½ cup brown sugar
3 Granny Smith apples, peeled, cored, and thinly sliced
2 ripe Bosc pears, peeled, cored, and thinly sliced
1 cup dried cranberries or raisins
1 cup chopped walnuts
2 teaspoons ground cinnamon
1 teaspoon ground coriander
¼ teaspoon freshly grated nutmeg
2 tablespoons freshly squeezed lemon juice
2 tablespoons milk
1 tablespoon granulated sugar
Confectioners' sugar

Lightly coat a baking sheet with nonstick cooking spray. Set aside.

In a food processor fitted with the plastic dough blade (or use a heavy-duty stand mixer), combine 1¾ cups of the bread flour with the yeast, salt, sugar, and orange zest. Add the sour cream, egg, and hot milk. Knead until mixture forms a soft dough. Add more flour as necessary, ¼ cup or so at a time. When the dough forms a ball and is no longer sticky, knead for an additional minute in the food processor, or 5 to 10 minutes in the mixer. Place dough in a zip-top freezer bag that has been coated with nonstick cooking spray, seal, and let double in volume, about 45 minutes.

Meanwhile, prepare the fruit. In a large skillet over medium heat melt the butter and stir in the brown sugar. Add the apples, pears, dried cranberries or raisins, walnuts, cinnamon, coriander, and nutmeg. Cook, stirring occasionally, until the fruit is tender and begins to caramelize, about 10 to 15 minutes. Remove from the heat and stir in the lemon juice.

Preheat the oven to 375°F.

Let the fruit mixture cool for 30 minutes. Punch down the doubled dough, then shape the dough into a 16-inch round. Place the dough on the prepared baking sheet. Spread the cooled fruit into a 12-inch circle in the center of the dough. Carefully pull the edges of the dough up and over the fruit, forming a 12-inch round. The formed galette will look very rustic and uneven. Lightly brush the dough with 2 tablespoons of milk and sprinkle with 1 tablespoon of granulated sugar.

Bake the galette for 35 to 45 minutes, or until the fruit is bubbly and the crust is golden brown. Remove to a wire rack to cool slightly. Sprinkle the folded-over crust with confectioners' sugar. Serve warm, cut into pie-shaped wedges.

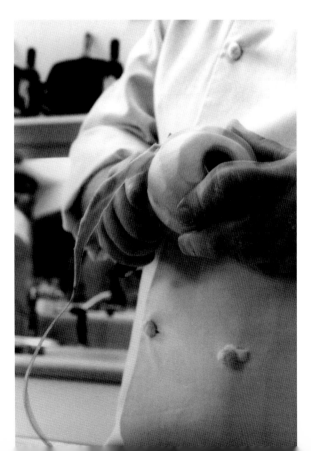

GINGERED PLUM CRISP

Plums are one of our most under-utilized fruits, which is a shame. They are not overly sweet, and lend a wonderful flavor to both savory entrees and desserts. The crunch of the topping comes from the addition of toasted barley cereal. You can substitute peaches, apples, pears, blueberries, or cherries for the plums.

SERVES 8

FRUIT MIXTURE

3 pounds purple plums, halved, pitted,
    and cut into ½-inch slices *
1½ cups sugar
⅓ cup cornstarch
4 tablespoons butter, melted
Juice and grated zest of 1 orange
3 tablespoons finely chopped,
    candied ginger
¼ teaspoon freshly grated nutmeg

CRISP TOPPING

1½ cups quick oats
¾ cup brown sugar
1 cup toasted barley cereal, such as
    Grape Nuts
½ cup chopped pecans
8 tablespoons (1 stick) butter, melted
½ teaspoon vanilla extract
¼ teaspoon almond extract

1 pound of fruit is equal to 4 to 5 plums, yielding about 2½ cups of fruit. You will need 8 to 9 cups of sliced plums for this recipe.

Preheat the oven to 350°F. Lightly butter a 8 x 12-inch baking dish and set aside.

In a large bowl combine the plums, sugar, cornstarch, 4 tablespoons of melted butter, orange juice and zest, candied ginger, and nutmeg. Toss the fruit to coat completely. Pour the contents of the bowl into the prepared baking dish.

In a medium bowl mix together the quick oats, brown sugar, toasted barley cereal, and pecans. Press this mixture evenly over the plums.

In a small bowl whisk together 8 tablespoons of melted butter, vanilla, and almond extract. Pour over the nut topping.

Bake for 50 to 60 minutes. Remove from the oven and let cool 20 minutes before serving. Serve warm or at room temperature.

VARIATION | Use 2 pounds of red plums and 1 pound of purple plums. The combination produces a beautiful amethyst color in the finished dish.

ORANGE ALMOND MADELEINES

The classic shell-shaped madeleine is a cross between a cake and a cookie. This recipe utilizes the mixing method of one of my favorite bakers, Rose Levy Beranbaum. If you don't have madeleine pans, you can bake these in mini-muffin tins, adding 2 to 3 minutes to the baking time.

MAKES | 3 DOZEN MADELEINES

3 tablespoons confectioners' sugar
1 tablespoon hot water
2 tablespoons orange juice concentrate
3 eggs
1 teaspoon vanilla extract
½ teaspoon almond extract
1¼ cups all-purpose flour
¾ cup sugar
¾ teaspoon baking powder
¼ teaspoon salt
Grated zest of 2 oranges
½ cup finely ground almonds
12 tablespoons (1½ sticks) butter, softened
Additional confectioners' sugar

SUGAR SYRUP

2 tablespoons sugar
¼ cup water
2 tablespoons Grand Marnier or other orange-flavored liqueur

Preheat the oven to 350°F. Lightly coat the madeleine molds with nonstick cooking spray. Set aside.

In a small mixing bowl combine the confectioners' sugar, hot water, and orange juice concentrate, whisking to dissolve. Mix in the eggs, vanilla, and almond extract.

In a heavy-duty stand mixer combine the flour, sugar, baking powder, salt, orange zest, and ground almonds. Mix on low speed for 30 seconds to blend. Add half of the egg mixture and all of the butter to the dry ingredients. Mix on low speed until the dry ingredients are moistened. Beat at medium-high speed for 1 minute. Scrape down the sides of the bowl and gradually add the remaining egg mixture in 2 batches, beating for 20 seconds after each addition. Scrape down the sides of the bowl. Transfer the batter into a gallon-sized zip-top freezer bag, close it securely, and cut off a small piece from the corner of the bag. Pipe the batter into the prepared molds, filling each about two-thirds full.

Bake for 10 to 12 minutes, or until a tester inserted into the center of the madeleines comes out clean and they spring back when lightly pressed in the centers. Let cool in the pans for about 1 minute, then unmold the madeleines onto a wire rack to cool completely.

While the madeleines are cooling, prepare the syrup: Mix together the sugar and the water in a small pan set over high heat. Bring to a full rolling boil, remove from the heat, and swirl in the Grand Marnier or other orange liqueur. Brush both sides of the cookies lightly with the syrup and sprinkle the shell side with additional confectioners' sugar before serving.

MAKE AHEAD | These madeleines will keep, tightly wrapped, for 1 week at room temperature, or for 3 months frozen.

GOLDEN NUT BISCOTTI

Biscotti, meaning "twice baked," is a natural accompaniment to morning coffee or afternoon tea. I like to pair this crunchy cookie with any of the fruit desserts in this book but especially the Caramel and Spice Citrus Fruit. For a delightful variation, dip one end or the bottom of the baked biscotti in melted chocolate and allow to harden.

MAKES | 3 DOZEN BISCOTTI

3 cups all-purpose flour
1 teaspoon baking powder
¼ teaspoon salt
1⅔ cups sugar
1 teaspoon aniseed
Grated zest of 1 orange
Grated zest of 1 lime
Grated zest of 1 lemon
4 tablespoons butter, softened
3 eggs plus 3 egg yolks, lightly beaten together
2 teaspoons vanilla extract
½ teaspoon almond extract
1½ cups sliced almonds
1 cup whole almonds (with skin on)
1 egg white, lightly beaten
2 tablespoons sugar mixed with ¼ teaspoon ground cinnamon

Preheat the oven to 350°F.

Lightly coat a baking sheet with nonstick cooking spray. Set aside.

In the bowl of an electric mixer combine the flour, baking powder, salt, sugar, aniseed, orange zest, lime zest, and lemon zest. Mix for 30 seconds. With the mixer running at medium speed, slowly beat in the butter, eggs and egg yolks, vanilla and almond extract. Do not overmix.

When the wet ingredients are almost incorporated, reduce the speed to low and add the sliced almonds and the whole almonds. Mix briefly just to blend. The mixture will be very crumbly. Scrape the dough onto a lightly floured counter. Knead into the dough any remaining ingredients from the bottom of the bowl.

With floured hands, divide the dough into 2 equal parts. Shape each piece into a log 10 inches long and 3½ inches in diameter. Flatten the logs until they are about ¾ inch thick. Place the logs on the lightly greased baking sheet. Brush each log with the egg white, then sprinkle with the cinnamon-sugar mixture. Bake the logs for 30 to 35 minutes.

Remove the logs and cool on the baking sheet for about 30 minutes, or until just warm. Carefully slip them off the baking sheet onto a cutting board. With a sharp chef's knife, cut the logs into ½-inch slices. Place the slices, cut side up, on the baking sheet. Reduce the oven temperature to 250°F. Return biscotti to the oven and toast for about 10 to 12 minutes. Turn the cookies over and toast for another 10 to 12 minutes, or until dry and golden. Transfer the biscotti to a wire rack and cool completely.

MAKE AHEAD | These keep at room temperature for several weeks, stored in an airtight container, or frozen, tightly wrapped, for 3 months.

CARAMEL AND SPICE CITRUS FRUIT

You can strain out the whole spices from the finished syrup, but I think they make a pretty presentation when left in. (Be sure not to eat any of the whole spices.) This is a totally fat-free dessert or brunch fruit salad and pairs very nicely with a slice of pound cake or a nutty biscotti.

SERVES 8

1½ cups sugar
½ cup light corn syrup
1½ cups water, divided
4 cinnamon sticks
10 to 12 whole allspice berries
4 to 6 whole cloves
1 whole nutmeg
1 whole star anise
¼ cup Grand Marnier or other orange-flavored liqueur
8 large navel oranges, peeled and cut into ½-inch slices
3 red grapefruit, peeled and cut into sections between the membranes, seeds removed
1 cup fresh blueberries

In a large, heavy-bottomed saucepan combine the sugar, corn syrup, and ½ cup of water. Heat over low heat until the sugar has dissolved. Turn the heat to high and continue to cook, using a pastry brush dipped in water to brush down any sugar crystals that might accumulate on the sides of the pan. Cook until the sugar syrup is a nice amber color and very thick, about 15 minutes. Remove the caramel from the heat and add the cinnamon sticks, allspice berries, cloves, nutmeg, and star anise. Stir gently for 1 minute. Return to the heat and carefully add the remaining 1 cup of water. (Wear an oven mitt, as the mixture can sometimes splatter.) Bring the mixture to a boil and cook for 2 minutes, or until all the mixture has returned to a liquid. If the caramel begins to brown too quickly, place the pot in a cake pan of cool water to slow the cooking and to lower the temperature of the caramel mixture. Remove from the heat and cool completely. Stir in the Grand Marnier.

In a pretty glass bowl alternately layer the orange slices, grapefruit wedges, and blueberries.

Pour the cooled, spiced syrup over the fruit, cover, and refrigerate for 6 hours before serving.

MAKE AHEAD | This dish can be made several days ahead of serving; in fact, the flavor intensifies the longer the dish sits.

VARIATION | For a creamy variation, omit the spices. Substitute 1½ cups of heavy cream for the final cup of water that is added to the cooked caramel. Return to the heat and cook for about 2 minutes, or until the mixture has returned to a liquid. Stir in 2 teaspoons of vanilla extract (or ¼ cup Grand Marnier, Amaretto, Frangelica, or Bailey's Irish Cream). Serve over ice cream or pound cake, or as a dip for fruit kabobs.

NOTE | To remove the peel and the pith (white part) of citrus fruits, use a sharp knife to slice off the top and the bottom of the fruit. This helps the fruit to stand up and also shows you the thickness of the peel. With the fruit sitting on a cutting board, slice downward just under the pith, removing the peel in sections. Working over a bowl to catch the juices, slice the fruit lengthwise into rounds or cut a V along each of the membranes and separate each segment. Continue until all the segments have been cut away. Squeeze any remaining membranes or pulp to extract all the juice.

FROSTED KAHLUA BROWNIES

These "one-bowl" brownies are the easiest (and best) I have ever tasted. I like the accents of Kahlua and cinnamon in every bite. This method of "icing" the brownies is a trick I learned from my grandmother. If so inclined, you can scatter the chopped nuts on top of the icing instead of folding them into the brownie batter.

MAKES ABOUT 3 DOZEN

2 cup sugar
1¼ cups all-purpose flour
⅔ cup unsweetened Dutch-process cocoa powder
½ teaspoon baking soda
½ teaspoon salt
½ teaspoon ground cinnamon
1 cup (2 sticks) butter, melted and cooled
4 eggs
¼ cup Kahlua or other coffee-flavored liqueur
2 teaspoons vanilla extract
1 cup chopped nuts (pecans, walnuts, or almonds)
1 cup mini-semisweet chocolate chips
2 (1 ounce) squares white chocolate, chopped

Preheat the oven to 350°F. Grease and flour a 13 x 9 x 2-inch baking dish and set aside.

In a large bowl combine the sugar, flour, cocoa powder, baking soda, salt, and cinnamon. Stir until blended. Add the melted butter, eggs, Kahlua, and vanilla. Stir until just blended. Fold in the chopped nuts. Pour the batter into the prepared baking dish. Bake for 40 to 45 minutes, or until the edges just begin to pull away from the sides of the dish.

Remove from the oven to a wire rack to cool. Sprinkle the semisweet chocolate chips on top of the hot brownies. Let them sit for about 5 minutes to melt, then spread over the brownies with a spatula. Sprinkle with the chopped white chocolate. When the white chocolate has softened, about 2 minutes, gently swirl them into the dark chocolate to create a marbled effect. Allow to cool for 2 hours before cutting.

ROSEMARY CARDAMOM SHORTBREAD COOKIES

Without a doubt, these are my "signature" cookies. People ask me to bring these for almost every special occasion. The addition of chopped fresh rosemary is the secret (and highly unorthodox) ingredient. These buttery cookies simply melt in your mouth.

MAKES ABOUT 3 DOZEN

1 cup (2 sticks) butter
1½ cups sugar, divided
1 teaspoon vanilla extract
2 teaspoons chopped fresh rosemary
1 teaspoon cardamom
½ teaspoon ground coriander
4 egg yolks
3 cups all-purpose flour, plus additional if needed
About 36 whole almonds or walnut halves

Preheat the oven to 350°F. Lightly grease 2 baking sheets and set aside.

In a heavy-duty stand mixer beat together the butter and ½ cup of the sugar until light and fluffy, about 3 minutes. Beat in the vanilla. Mix in the rosemary, cardamom, and coriander. Add the egg yolks, one at a time, alternating with the flour. The dough should be soft but not sticky. Add more flour if needed.

With your fingers, pull off walnut-sized pieces of dough and quickly roll into balls in the palm of your hands. Lightly flour your hands if needed. Place the remaining cup of sugar in a shallow pie plate and roll each ball in the sugar to coat. Place the balls about 1½ inches apart on the baking sheets. Press one almond or walnut half in the center of each ball.

Bake the cookies until lightly browned, about 18 to 22 minutes. Transfer them to a wire rack to cool.

MAKE AHEAD The cookies can be stored up to 1 week in an airtight container or frozen, tightly wrapped, for up to 2 months.

THE ABSOLUTE BEST, ALL-TIME FAVORITE CHOCOLATE CHIP COOKIES

I received this recipe by fax from an anonymous source, very mysterious and secretive. It is supposed to be the "classified" recipe of one of the "gourmet" chocolate chip cookies sold in specialty shops around the country. All I know is that it is the best chocolate chip cookie I have ever made. I think you will agree.

MAKES | ABOUT 4 DOZEN COOKIES

1 cup (2 sticks) butter, softened

1 cup sugar

1 cup brown sugar

2 eggs, lightly beaten

2 teaspoons vanilla extract

2 cups all-purpose flour

2 cups oatmeal, processed in a food processor to a fine powder

½ teaspoon salt

1 teaspoon baking powder

1 teaspoon baking soda

¼ teaspoon ground cinnamon

Freshly grated nutmeg

1½ cups semisweet chocolate chips

½ cup grated bittersweet chocolate (not unsweetened)

2 cup chopped walnuts

¾ cup shredded coconut, lightly toasted in a 350°F oven for 5 minutes (optional)

Preheat the oven to 375°F. Lightly coat 2 baking sheets with nonstick cooking spray. Set aside.

In a heavy-duty stand mixer combine the butter and the sugars. Beat until light and fluffy, about 2 minutes. Add the eggs and vanilla and mix well.

On a piece of waxed paper, sift together the flour, processed oatmeal, salt, baking powder, baking soda, cinnamon, and nutmeg to taste. Add to the butter-egg mixture and mix until all ingredients are moistened. Stir in the semisweet chocolate chips, grated chocolate, and chopped walnuts. Add the toasted coconut if desired.

Shape mixture into balls of 1 to 1½ tablespoons each. Place about 2 inches apart on the prepared baking sheets. Bake for 12 to 14 minutes, or until the cookies are golden brown. Remove from the oven and let sit on the baking sheet a couple of minutes. Carefully transfer the cookies to a wire rack to cool completely.

MAKE AHEAD | Store in an airtight container for 1 week, or freeze for up to 3 months.

GERMAN CHOCOLATE TARTLETS

These delightful "two-bite" tartlets are perfect for ending a large meal when you crave just a taste of something sweet. They taste like miniature pecan pies, but with the subtle taste of chocolate and coconut added.

MAKES | ABOUT 4 DOZEN TARTLETS

PASTRY DOUGH

2 cups all-purpose flour

⅓ cup confectioners' sugar

1 (8 ounce) package cream cheese, cut into cubes and chilled

12 tablespoons (1½ sticks) butter, cut into cubes and chilled

½ teaspoon vanilla extract

FILLING

1 cup brown sugar

2 eggs, well beaten

1 tablespoon all-purpose flour

⅛ teaspoon ground cinnamon

3 tablespoons butter, softened

2 teaspoons vanilla extract

1 cup finely chopped pecans

½ cup shredded coconut

4 ounces German baking chocolate, finely chopped

Preheat the oven to 350°F. Lightly coat four 12-count mini-muffin tins with nonstick cooking spray and set aside.

In a food processor combine the flour, confectioners' sugar, cream cheese, butter, and vanilla. Blend thoroughly just until the mixture forms a ball. Divide the dough into 48 equal pieces and roll each piece into a ball. (If dough is too soft to handle, chill briefly.) Place each ball into the prepared mini-muffin cups and press the dough with your fingers into the bottom and sides of the little cups. (This job is so much easier if you have a "tart tamper" gadget, dipped lightly in flour). Place tins in the refrigerator to chill while you prepare the filling.

In a large bowl mix together the brown sugar, eggs, flour, cinnamon, butter, and vanilla. Beat with a wooden spoon until smooth. Stir in the chopped pecans, coconut, and German chocolate.

Carefully spoon the filling into the muffin cups so they are not quite full. Bake for 25 to 30 minutes, or until the filling is set. Set the tins on a wire rack to cool for 10 minutes. Remove tartlets from the pans and finish cooling completely on the wire rack.

MAKE AHEAD | The tartlets freeze very well, tightly wrapped, for up to 3 months.

PERFECT BUTTER POUND CAKE

I adapted this technique for mixing the batter from a method used by Rose Levy Beranbaum, author of *The Cake Bible*. The addition of the sour cream and the vanilla seeds provides a wonderful moistness and texture to the finished cake.

MAKES | ONE 9 X 5-INCH CAKE

2½ cups cake flour
1¼ cups sugar
1 tablespoon baking powder
½ teaspoon salt
1 cup (2 sticks) butter, softened
⅓ cup sour cream
5 eggs, lightly beaten
1 vanilla bean, split lengthwise, seeds scraped and removed
2 teaspoons vanilla extract

Preheat the oven to 325°F. Lightly grease and flour a 9 x 5 x 3-inch loaf pan, line the bottom of the pan with strips of waxed paper cut to fit, and grease and flour the paper. Set aside.

In a heavy-duty stand mixer combine the flour, sugar, baking powder, and salt. Mix on low speed for 30 seconds to thoroughly combine the dry ingredients. Add the softened butter and the sour cream, along with half of the beaten eggs. Increase the speed to medium and beat for 1 minute, scraping down the sides of the bowl. Add the remaining eggs, the vanilla bean seeds, and the vanilla. Beat for 30 seconds. Pour the batter into the prepared pan.

Bake for 1¼ to 1½ hours, or until a toothpick inserted into the center comes out clean. (Cover the top of the cake loosely with aluminum foil if it begins to brown too quickly.) Place the pan on a wire rack and let the cake cool for 10 minutes. Gently loosen the edges of the cake with a thin knife or spatula. Remove the cake from the pan, carefully peel away the waxed paper strips, and cool completely.

PUMPKIN SPICE ROULADE

I keep several of these roulades, or "rolled cakes," tightly wrapped in my freezer at all times. At the beginning of the meal I simply unwrap and slice however many servings I need. By dessert, they are perfectly defrosted and ready to enjoy. Try this frozen too. It tastes like a delicious ice-cream cake.

SERVES 8 TO 10

3 eggs, separated
½ cup brown sugar
⅔ cup canned solid pack pumpkin (not pumpkin pie filling)
½ teaspoon baking soda
½ teaspoon salt
¾ teaspoon ground cinnamon
¾ teaspoon ground ginger
¾ cup all-purpose flour
½ cup sugar
½ teaspoon almond extract
Confectioners' sugar

FILLING

2 (8 ounce) packages cream cheese, at room temperature
¾ cup confectioners' sugar
2 tablespoons butter, at room temperature
3 tablespoons Grand Marnier or other orange-flavored liqueur (or 1 tablespoon vanilla extract)
Grated zest of 2 oranges
Additional confectioners' sugar
Additional orange zest (in strips, not grated)

Preheat oven to 375°F. Lightly grease and flour a 15 x 10 x 1-inch jelly roll pan. Line with waxed paper. Grease and flour the waxed paper. Set aside.

Place egg yolks and brown sugar in a large bowl. With an electric mixer on medium-high speed, beat until light and fluffy, about 2 to 3 minutes. Add the pumpkin to the mixture and combine well. Set aside.

In a medium bowl sift together the baking soda, salt, cinnamon, ginger, and flour. Stir into pumpkin mixture until just combined. In a clean, large bowl beat egg whites until soft peaks begin to form. Add sugar and almond extract and beat until peaks are glossy and hold their shape. Fold ⅓ of the egg whites into the pumpkin mixture to lighten. Add the pumpkin mixture back into the remaining egg whites and fold gently until just combined.

Pour into prepared pan and bake for 12 to 15 minutes, or until cake springs back when lightly pressed. Invert pan onto a tea towel dusted with confectioners' sugar. Peel off the waxed paper. Sprinkle the cake with additional confectioners' sugar. While the cake is still hot, roll it up lengthwise, using the tea towel as you roll. Allow rolled cake to cool.

While the cake is cooling, make the filling: Beat together the cream cheese, confectioners' sugar, butter, Grand Marnier, and grated orange zest. Unroll the cooled cake and spread the cream cheese filling to within ½ inch of the edges of the cake. Reroll the cake and chill for at least 2 hours.

When ready to serve, place the roulade, seam side down, on a serving platter and sprinkle with the additional confectioners' sugar and orange zest.

MAKE AHEAD | The roulade freezes well, tightly wrapped in foil, for several months. It can be sliced frozen or thawed in the refrigerator.

TOTALLY DECADENT FUDGE CAKE

I received a version of this recipe in the mail with one of those offers to join a recipe cooking club. I adapted it to make it easier (and to use more chocolate, of course). I like these cakes because I can make two at once and either freeze the second for another occasion or give it as a gift. I have included instructions for glazing these cakes, but they are equally good plain.

MAKES 2 SMALL CAKES

2 sticks butter, softened

1½ cups sugar

4 eggs

½ teaspoon baking soda

1 cup buttermilk

2½ cups all-purpose flour sifted together with ¼ cup unsweetened Dutch-process cocoa powder

1 cup semisweet mini-chocolate chips

2 (1 ounce) squares white chocolate, chopped

2 (4 ounce) bars German baking chocolate, melted and cooled

⅓ cup chocolate syrup, such as Hershey's

1 tablespoon vanilla extract

Preheat the oven to 300°F. Grease and flour two 4-cup-capacity pans, such as small Bundt or brioche pans or pudding molds. Set aside.

In a heavy-duty stand mixer beat the butter and the sugar at medium speed until the mixture is light and fluffy, about 2 minutes. Add the eggs, one at a time, beating well after each addition. In a measuring cup with a 2-cup capacity, dissolve the baking soda in the buttermilk. Add the flour-cocoa mixture to the creamed butter-sugar mixture in 3 batches, alternating with the buttermilk mixture and beginning and ending with the dry ingredients. Add the mini-chocolate chips, white chocolate, melted German chocolate, chocolate syrup, and vanilla, mixing until just blended. Do not overbeat. Divide the batter between the prepared pans and place pans in the center of the oven for about 1 hour and 25 to 35 minutes, or until a toothpick inserted into the center of the cakes comes out clean and the cakes spring back when touched. Invert the cakes immediately onto a wire rack and let cool completely.

NOTE For an easy frosting and decorating option, in a 1-quart zip-top freezer bag combine 1 cup of chocolate chips and 1 teaspoon of shortening and seal tightly. In a separate freezer bag place 4 (1ounce) squares of chopped white chocolate and seal tightly. Place the bags in a bowl and cover with barely simmering water. Allow the chocolate to sit in the bags in the water until it begins to melt, about 3 minutes. With your hands, knead the chocolate in the bags until smooth and creamy. With scissors, snip a small opening out of the corner of each bag. Pipe or drizzle the melted chocolate over the cooled cakes.

MAKE AHEAD This cake freezes well, without the chocolate glazes, for about 3 months.

FRESH AND DRIED APPLE SPICE CAKE WITH GINGERED SOUR CREAM TOPPING

As this bakes, the kitchen is infused with the wonderful scent of sweet spices. In fact, the hardest part about making this moist apple cake is waiting for it to cool before slicing into it.

MAKES ONE 13 X 9-INCH CAKE

CAKE

1½ cups all-purpose flour

½ cup whole-wheat flour

½ cup rolled oats or oatmeal (not quick cooking)

1½ cups brown sugar

2 teaspoons baking soda

1 teaspoon baking powder

½ teaspoon salt

2 teaspoons ground cinnamon

1 teaspoon ground ginger

½ teaspoon allspice

1 cup chunky applesauce

1 (8 ounce) carton sour cream

3 eggs, lightly beaten

4 tablespoons butter, melted

1 cup diced dried apples

2 Granny Smith apples, peeled, cored, and grated

½ cup dark raisins

½ cup golden raisins

½ cup walnut pieces

1 teaspoon vanilla extract

GINGERED SOUR CREAM TOPPING

1 (16 ounce) carton sour cream

¼ cup brown sugar

½ teaspoon ground cinnamon

1 teaspoon vanilla extract

⅓ cup chopped candied ginger

Preheat the oven to 325°F.

Coat a 13 x 9 x 2-inch baking pan with a nonstick cooking spray that contains added flour (such as Baker's Joy). In a large bowl combine the all-purpose flour, whole-wheat flour, oats, brown sugar, baking soda, baking powder, salt, cinnamon, ginger, and allspice. Set aside.

In a medium bowl whisk together the applesauce, sour cream, eggs, and melted butter. Pour this into the bowl with the dry ingredients and stir until well combined.

Fold in the diced dried apples, grated apples, dark and golden raisins, walnuts, and vanilla. Pour into the prepared pan and bake for 40 to 45 minutes, or until the cake is a nice golden brown and just begins to pull away from the sides of the pan. Cool completely in the pan on a wire rack.

While the cake is baking, make the topping. In a small bowl whisk together the topping ingredients. Cover and refrigerate.

To serve, cut into 24 squares and top each piece of cake with a dollop of Gingered Sour Cream Topping.

NOTES Crystallized, or candied, ginger is less expensive when bought in an Asian market.

If you don't want to make the topping for the cake, omit the golden raisins and stir ⅓ cup of chopped, candied ginger into the batter. Bake as directed. Dust with confectioners' sugar before serving.

PINEAPPLE UPSIDE-DOWN GINGERBREAD

Unlike the plain butter cake used in traditional pineapple upside-down cake recipes, this spicy gingerbread is as flavorful as the carmelized fruit and nut topping it accompanies. More rustic in appearance than the usual pineapple upside-down cake, it is suitable for either an impromptu gathering of friends or a more elegant sit-down dinner.

SERVES | 8

TOPPING

4 tablespoons butter
½ cup dark brown sugar
1 (16 ounce) can pineapple chunks in natural juice, drained
⅔ cup chopped pecans

CAKE

8 tablespoons (1 stick) butter, softened
½ cup dark brown sugar
1 egg, lightly beaten
¼ cup molasses
1½ cups all-purpose flour
2 teaspoons ground ginger
1 teaspoon ground cinnamon
¼ teaspoon freshly grated nutmeg
¼ teaspoon ground cloves
¾ teaspoon baking soda
¼ teaspoon salt
⅓ cup boiling water mixed with 1 teaspoon vanilla extract

Preheat the oven to 350°F.

Make the topping: Lightly coat a 10-inch-round, well-seasoned cast-iron skillet with nonstick cooking spray. In the skillet melt 4 tablespoons of butter over medium heat and add ½ cup of brown sugar, stirring until the sugar melts. Add the chunked pineapple and chopped pecans. Cook over low heat for 1 to 2 minutes to glaze the pineapple. Set aside.

Make the cake: In a large bowl with a hand-held mixer, beat together 8 tablespoons of butter and ½ cup of brown sugar until light and fluffy, about 1 minute. Add the egg and molasses and continue to beat until well blended. On a piece of waxed paper, sift together the flour, ginger, cinnamon, nutmeg, cloves, baking soda, and salt. Gently fold the flour mixture into the butter-sugar mixture in 2 batches, alternating with the boiling water and vanilla. Do not overmix.

Pour the batter over the topping and bake for 35 to 40 minutes, or until the cake is springy to the touch. Remove the skillet to a wire rack to cool for 5 minutes, then invert the cake onto a serving plate. Slice into wedges and serve warm.

VARIATION | Substitute 2 cups of peeled and coarsely grated tart apples, sweet pears, or peeled and diced peaches for the pineapple.

EXTRAORDINARY RICOTTA CHEESECAKE

This is the creamiest cheesecake I have ever tasted. The recipe was shared with me by a friend's grandmother, a delightful woman from Naples who now lives in Little Italy in New York City. She swore that this cheesecake would never crack on top. And you know what? She's absolutely right!

SERVES 10 TO 12

CRUST

1 cup finely ground pecans
1½ cups gingersnap cookie crumbs
1 cup confectioners' sugar
6 tablespoons butter, melted

FILLING

4 eggs
3 tablespoons all-purpose flour
¾ cup sugar
1 (16 ounce) container whole-milk or part-skim ricotta cheese, drained
2 (8 ounce) packages cream cheese, softened
⅓ cup sour cream
1 tablespoon vanilla extract
Mint sprigs and seasonal berries (optional)

Preheat the oven to 375°F. Lightly grease a 10-inch springform pan and set aside.

In a large bowl combine the pecans, gingersnap crumbs, confectioners' sugar, and melted butter. Pack the crust evenly on the bottom and halfway up the sides of the springform pan. Bake the crust for 12 to 15 minutes. Remove to a wire rack to cool completely.

With an electric mixer beat the eggs, flour, and sugar until well blended and light, about 3 minutes. Slowly beat in the ricotta cheese, cream cheese, sour cream, and vanilla. Beat until well combined, about 1 minute more. Pour the batter into the prepared crust.

Place in the preheated 375°F oven and bake for 15 minutes. Reduce the heat to 250°F and continue baking for 60 to 70 minutes, or until the center is barely set. The cake will continue to set as it cools. Turn the oven off, and with a wooden spoon handle prop the door slightly ajar. Cool cake in the oven for 2 hours. Remove and finish cooling on a wire rack.

When the cheesecake is cool to the touch, wrap and refrigerate overnight.

When ready to serve, slice into wedges and serve garnished with fresh berries and sprigs of mint.

NOTES | To soften cream cheese quickly and easily, place in a zip-top freezer bag and submerge in hot water for 2 minutes. Knead through the bag until pliable.

To slice the cheesecake into neat, uniform slices, dip a sharp knife into hot water before making each slice. Wipe the knife clean with a kitchen towel after each slice.

STRAWBERRIES BALSAMICO

Serve this unique flavor combination of fresh fruit and sweet balsamic vinegar with a crunchy nut biscotti or buttery pound cake – or simply on its own with a medium dry champagne. Bravo!

SERVES 8

4 cups very ripe strawberries, hulled and cut in half lengthwise
¼ cup brown sugar
¼ cup good quality balsamic vinegar
½ teaspoon black pepper

In a large nonreactive bowl gently toss together the strawberries and brown sugar until the sugar has dissolved. Stir in the balsamic vinegar and pepper. Let sit for 1 hour at room temperature, stirring every 15 minutes.

Refrigerate overnight if desired.

NOTE To easily hull a strawberry, take an ordinary plastic drinking straw and insert it through the bottom, or blossom, end of the berry, pushing the cap out at the other end.

SUGGESTED MENUS

Sorrel Watercress Soup
Sizzling Spring Ginger Salmon
Couscous with Asparagus
Sour Cream and Chive Bread
German Chocolate Tartlets

Arugula, Pine Nut, and Parmesan Salad
Garlic Pan-Roasted Shrimp
White Beans with Tarragon and Nicoise Olives
Parmesan Pepper Wreath
Parisian Galette with Spiced Fruit

Roasted Garlic and Onion Soup with Fennel
Lemon-Marinated Leg of Lamb with Mint Gremolata
Wild Rice with Portobello Mushrooms
Walnut and Black Olive Fougasse
Champagne-Poached Pears

Gingered Sweet Potato and Apple Vichyssoise
Balsamic Roasted Chicken with Garlic and Fresh Herbs
Minted Green Beans with Red Onion and Red Pepper
Wild Rice Muffins
Strawberries Balsamico with Golden Nut Biscotti

Leek and Stilton Cheese Soufflé
Asian Barbecued Turkey Breast with Fiery Harissa Sauce
Braised Red Cabbage with Apples
Puff Pastry Cheese Twists
Pear, Black Pepper, and Walnut Tart

SUGGESTED MENUS

Pecan-Smoked Trout Spread with Lime Cumin Parmesan Wafers
Japanese Spinach Salad with Sesame Ginger Vinaigrette
Herb-Crusted Beef Tenderloin with Sunshine Béarnaise Sauce
Oven-Browned French Fries with Fennel and Dijon
Green Beans Pistou
Totally Decadent Fudge Cake

Creamy Crab, Parmesan, and Chipotle Dip
Blood Orange and Red Onion Salad with Feta Vinaigrette
Phyllo-Layered Vegetable Strudel or Succulent Seafood Jambalaya
The Absolute Best, All-Time Favorite Chocolate Chip Cookies

Winter Root Vegetable Tart with Three Cheeses
Mixed Baby Greens with Champagne Raspberry Vinaigrette
Vegetable Ribbons with Horseradish Lemon Butter
Orange Almond Madeleines

Classic Caesar Salad
Molasses- and Cider-Basted Loin of Pork with
Southwestern Apple and Red Chile Chutney
Indian Basmati Rice with Dried Fruit or
Banana Pepper, Squash, and Corn Pudding
Very Berry Nonfat Frozen Yogurt

Tri-Mustard Pork with Zesty Black Bean Salsa
Oven-Roasted New Potato and Artichoke Salad
Sweet Potato Buttermilk Biscuits
Frosted Kahlua Brownies

SUGGESTED MENUS

Beautiful Bouquet Salad with Cilantro Lime Vinaigrette
Ratatouille Gratin
Savory Herb and Sunflower Seed Bread
Caramel and Spice Citrus Fruit with
Rosemary Cardamom Shortbread Cookies

Marbled Melon Soup
Turkey Piccata
Lemon and Saffron Risotto with Asparagus Tips
Rhubarb and Peach Cobbler or Caramel and Walnut Sticky Buns

Classic Cod Cakes with Jalapeño Tartar Sauce or
Blue Cornmeal Catfish Fillets with Toasted Pecan Butter
Crushed Red Potatoes with Bitter Greens
Garlic-Thyme Corn Muffins
Pumpkin Spice Roulade

Penne Baked with Exotic Mushrooms
Zucchini Ripieni
Rosemary and Garlic Breadsticks
Double Dutch Chocolate Meringue Pie

Szechwan Chicken and Shrimp Brochettes
Thai-Style Noodles with Crunchy Vegetables
Spicy Rapini Eleanora
Extraordinary Ricotta Cheesecake

Provençal Tapenade Croûtes
Moroccan Lemon Chicken
Parmesan Garlic Mashed Potatoes
Pineapple Upside-Down Gingerbread

ACKNOWLEDGMENTS

The ultimate success of any project relies on the constant influences of others. This undertaking is no exception, for it would have been impossible without the contributions of many people.

Special thanks to my parents, Jan and Ray Overton, for being the guiding force in my life and for instilling in me their faith, work ethic and love for all people. You truly made a difference in who I am today. And to my Granny Lou, who first showed me around the kitchen.

I owe a debt of gratitude to Nathalie Dupree for being such a strong presence in my life and career, and for unselfishly teaching me all about the food industry. Thanks also to Julia Child, for paving the way for the rest of us!

Thank you to Susan Montgomery, my assistant, kitchen manager and dear friend. Your dedication to the success of this book and the cooking school are priceless. And so is your friendship! And to Mike Montgomery, thanks for always being so understanding and for offering your invaluable business advice.

Love and admired appreciation to my best "buds" in New York, Kay Ponder and Nancy McKenna. Thanks for your mothering (I've just grown to accept it) and the way you keep me humble. Now, if I could only teach Kay to cook. . .

I want to especially acknowledge all the people at Longstreet Press who are behind this book. To my editor, Suzanne De Galan, thank you for making my words flow and my prose make sense, and for your caring attention to the smallest detail. I'll proudly say it again, you are the best. To Burtch Hunter, for his intricate eye and tremendous artistic talent in designing the overall look and feel of this unique cookbook, I am forever grateful. To Sherry Wade, a wonderful assistant editor, for her tireless commitment and friendly encouragement in helping to see this project through to completion. And special thanks to Chuck Perry, Steve Gracie and Marge McDonald for their continued support and faith in my work.

Thank you, thank you, thank you to a very accomplished photographer, Jerry Burns, and his

ACKNOWLEDGMENTS

assistants Guy Welch, Luis Mendoza and David "Morty" Troy. Your images are truly inspired. Working with you all was the first time I ever actually enjoyed a photo shoot! As always, love and special thanks to my longtime friend and very talented food stylist, Will Deller. I only need to tell you what I want in the photographs, and you create the likeness without fuss or pretense. Special thanks to the folks at Williams-Sonoma for the many props and platters used in the photographs. Thank you to Vicky Murphy of Inland Seafood for providing the seafood used in the photographs and in the testing of some of the recipes. Thank you Will, my assistant Susan, Jane Fasse and Carolyn Packard for preparing the dishes for the camera and for doing whatever is asked to help make my books and my cooking classes a success.

My endless gratitude to everyone at Le Creuset of America, Inc., especially Finn Schjorring, Faye Gooding, Lacey Devereaux and Janis Faciszewski, for supporting the source of these recipes, my cooking school. None of this would have been possible without your dedicated commitment to excellence in the culinary world. Special thanks to Mark Lindsay, Monique Gainsley and Barbara Fogle for constantly offering their invaluable hands-on service to the school.

Special thanks to Dee Beaumarriage for sharing her computer knowledge so freely and for saving me from disaster on several occasions. And for teaching me how to "double space" (my editor loves you for this).

On a personal note, thank you to Brian Seifried, my confidante and best friend in the whole world, and to the rest of our gang: Stephen Barnwell, Ken Folds, Clint Bearden, Alan Vineyard, Donald Alexander and Heyward Young. You guys are the best food "guinea pigs" ever, and your laughter and friendship help to keep me sane.

Thank you to all the apprentices who work so devotedly behind the scenes, setting up, assisting me and testing and retesting the recipes for my classes and books. And finally, my lasting gratitude to the nearly 10,000 students I have taught over the years. Without your continued support, desire to learn and enthusiasm to master the kitchen, *Layers of Flavors* would be nothing more than an unfulfilled fantasy.

BIBLIOGRAPHY

Bailey, Lee. *Lee Bailey's Soup Meals*: *Main Event Soups in Year-Round Menus*. New York: Crown Publishing Group, 1989.

Beranbaum, Rose Levy. *The Cake Bible*. New York: William Morrow and Company, Inc., 1988.

Child, Julia. *The Way to Cook*. New York: Knopf, 1989.

Corriher, Shirley D. *Cookwise*. New York: William Morrow and Company, Inc., 1997.

Cutler, Carol. *Catch of the Day: A Fish Cookbook*. Mount Vernon, N.Y.: Consumer Reports Books, 1990.

Dupree, Nathalie. *Nathalie Dupree Cooks for Family and Friends*. New York: Morrow, 1991.

_____. *Nathalie Dupree's Southern Memories*: Recipes and Reminiscences. New York: Clarkson Potter, Inc., 1993.

Eckhardt, Linda West. *Bread in Half the Time*: *Use Your Microwave and Food Processor to Make Real Yeast Bread in 90 Minutes*. New York: Crown Publishers, Inc., 1991.

Ferrary, Jeanette and Louise Fiszer. *Sweet Onions and Sour Cherries: A Cookbook for Market Day*. New York: Simon and Schuster, 1992.

Fobel, Jim. *Jim Fobel's Big Flavors*. New York: Crown Publishers, 1995.

Fong-Torres, Shirley. *In The Chinese Kitchen with Shirley Fong-Torres*. Berkeley, Calif.: Pacific View Press, 1993.

Herbst, Sharon Tyler. *The New Food Lover's Companion: Comprehensive Definitions of Over 3,000 Food, Wine, and Culinary Terms*. New York: Barron's Educational Series, 1995.

Hewitt, Gillian, ed. *American Food: A Celebration*. San Francisco: Collins Publishers, 1993.

Kimball, Christopher. *The Cook's Bible: The Best of American Home Cooking*. Boston: Little, Brown and Company, 1996.

BIBLIOGRAPHY

Loomis, Susan Herrman. *The Great American Seafood Cookbook*. New York: Workman Publishing, 1988.

Malgieri, Nick. *Nick Malgieri's Perfect Pastry*. New York: Macmillan Publishing Co., 1989.

_____. *How to Bake*. New York: HarperCollins Publishers, 1995.

McGee, Harold. *On Food and Cooking: The Science and Lore of the Kitchen*. New York: Scribners, 1984.

Miller, Mark. *Coyote Cafe*. Berkeley, Calif.: Ten Speed Press, 1989.

Montague, Prosper. *New Larousse Gastronomique*. Twickenham, England: Hamlyn, 1960.

O'Neill, Molly. *New York Cookbook*. New York: Workman Publishing, 1992.

Prudhomme, Paul. *Chef Paul Prudhomme's Louisiana Kitchen*. New York: Morrow, 1984.

Rogers, Mara Reid. *The South the Beautiful Cookbook*. San Francisco: Collins Publishers, 1996.

_____. *The Instant Ethnic Cook*. New York: Lake Isle Press, 1993.

Schmidt, Stephen. *Master Recipes: A Complete Cooking Course*. New York: Ballantine Books, 1987.

Shulman, Martha Rose. *Mediterranean Light*. New York: Bantam Books, 1989.

Southern Living. *The Southern Living Cookbook*. Birmingham, Ala.: Oxmoor House, 1987

Spear, Ruth. *East Hampton Cookbook of Menus and Recipes*. New York: Dell Publishing, 1988.

Wells, Patricia. *Trattoria*. New York: Morrow, 1993.

Willan, Anne. *La Varenne Pratique: The Complete Illustrated Guide to the Techniques, Ingredients and Tools of Classic Modern Cooking*. New York: Crown Publishing Group, 1989.

INDEX

INDEX

INDEX